Now I Know!

1

Learning to read

Workbook

Peter Loveday and Tessa Lochowski

Contents

1 What do you find in schools?

1 **Draw.**

What do you know?

2 1-1 BBC **Watch the video. Check (✓) the things you see.**

3 **What's in your backpack? Check (✓).**

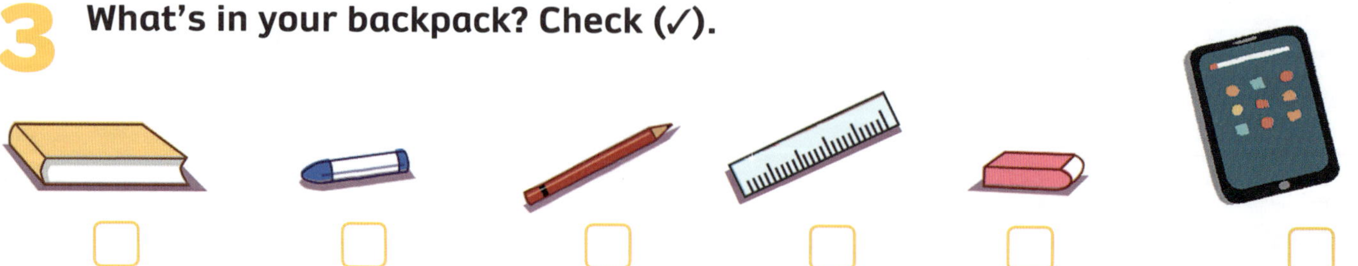

Vocabulary 1

1 01 **Listen and color.**

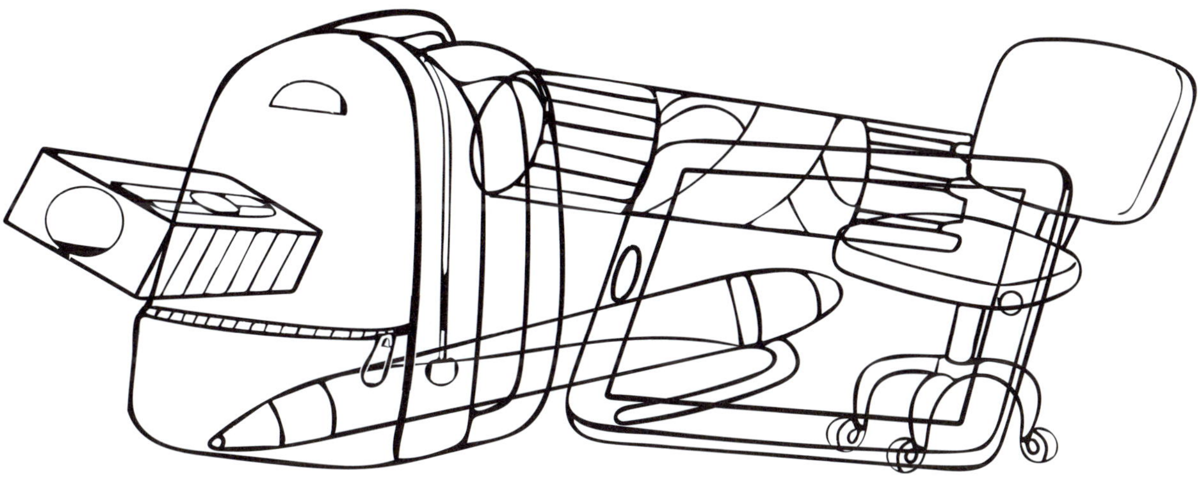

2 Match and say.

1

4

2

5

3

6

d

a

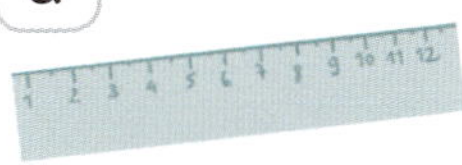

b

e

f

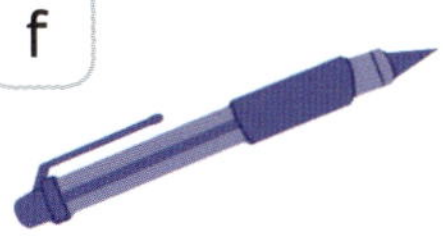

c

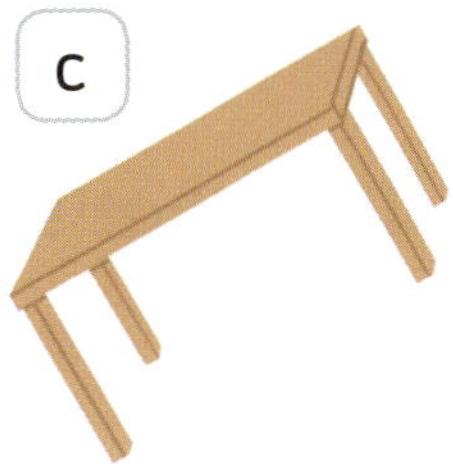

3 Trace and say.

1

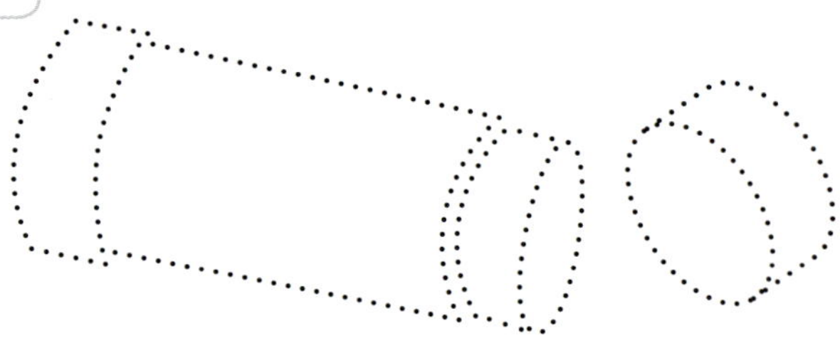

2

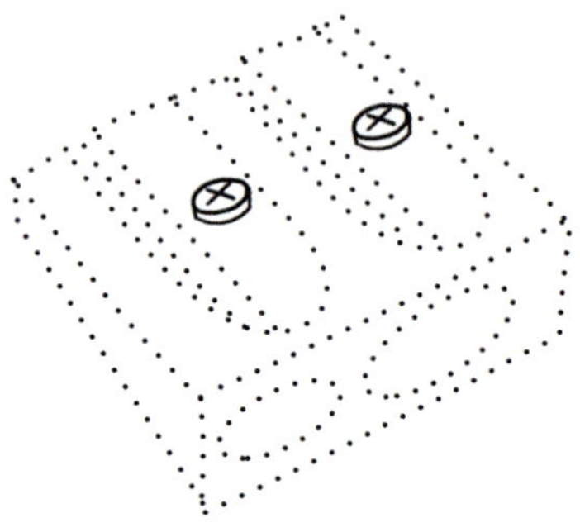

3

4

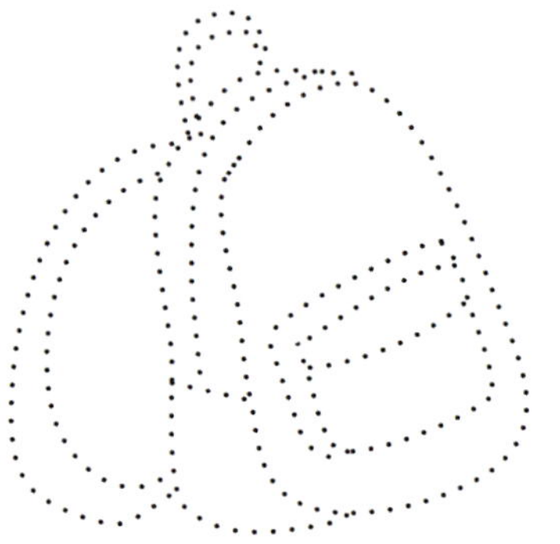

Vocabulary challenge

4 Listen and check (✓).

02

5 Talk in pairs. What's in your classroom?

Story 1

1 Listen and check (✓).

03

1

2

2 What's in the story? Check (✓).

3 Draw your classroom.

Grammar 1

1 Listen and check (✓).

04

1

3
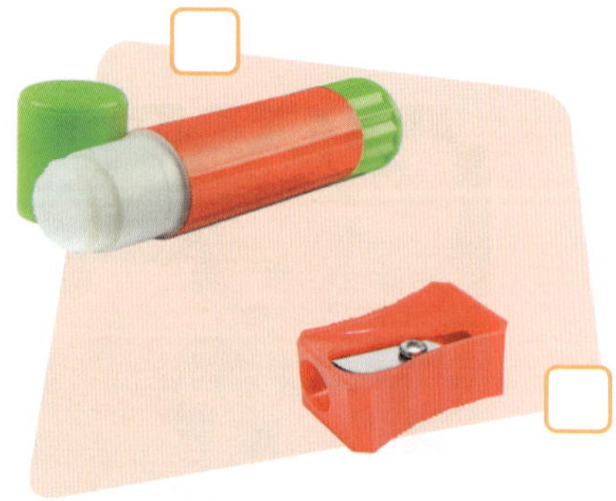

2

4
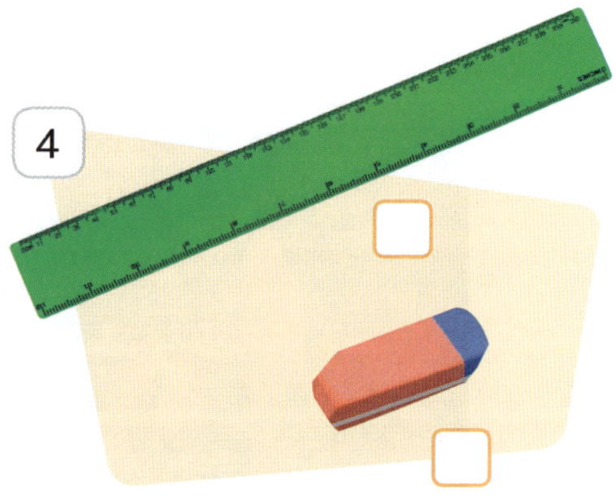

2 Listen and check (✓) or cross (✗).

05

1

3

2

4

3 Ask and answer in pairs.

4 Say. Then listen.

06

1

3

2

4

Vocabulary 2

1 Listen and check (✓) or cross (✗).

07

1

3

2

4

2 What's in your school library? Check (✓).

3 Listen and number.

08

Numbers 1–10

4 Look and match. Then say.

1 2 3 4 5 6 7 8 9 10

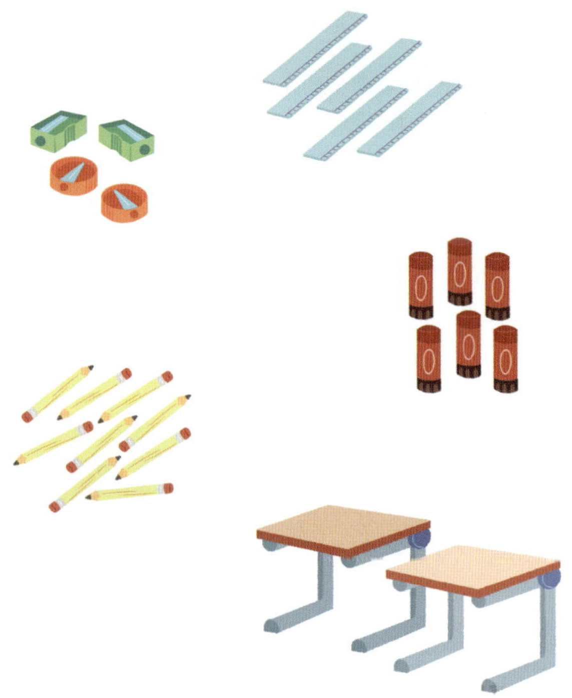

5 Count and circle the number.

2 1

5 4

6 3

5 7

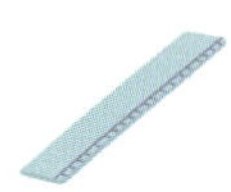

9 8

8 10

Story 2

1 Number the pictures. Listen to the story.

09

2 Listen and say *Yes* or *No*.

10

3 What do you like at school? Check (✓).

Grammar 2

1 Listen and color.

11

2 Trace and say.

1

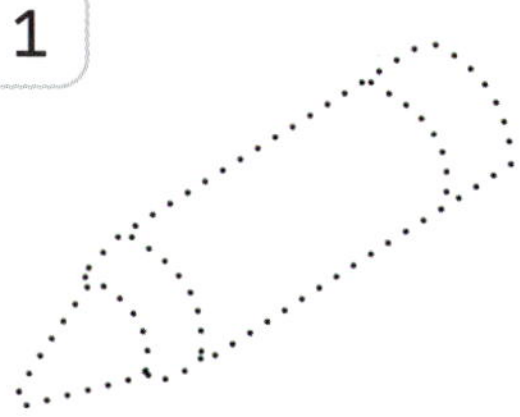

2

3

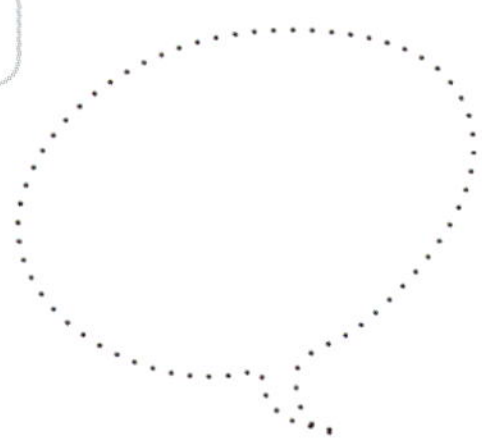

4

3 Listen and number.

12

4 Draw your favorite school activity.

Phonics

1 Trace the letters.

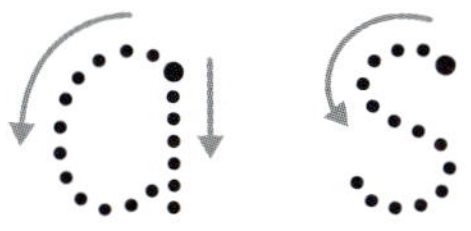

2 13 Listen, find, and check (✓).

a ✓ s ✓

Now I Know

1 Match and say.

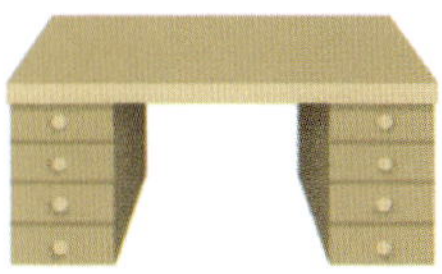

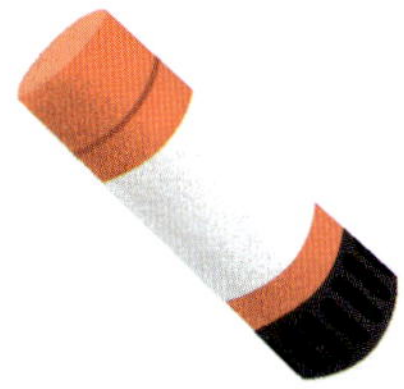

2 Listen and follow.

14

3 Ask and answer in pairs. What's this?

1
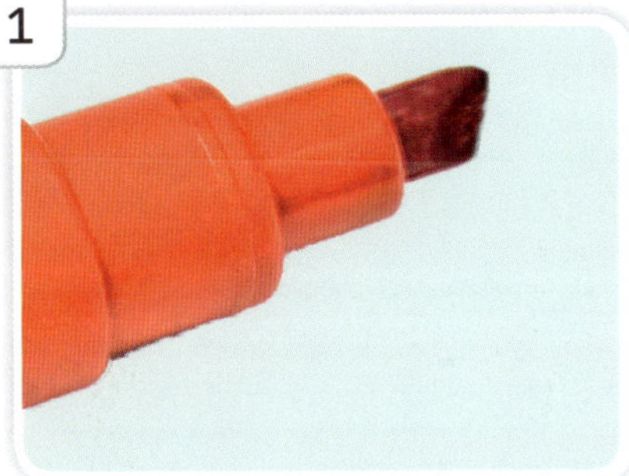

3

2
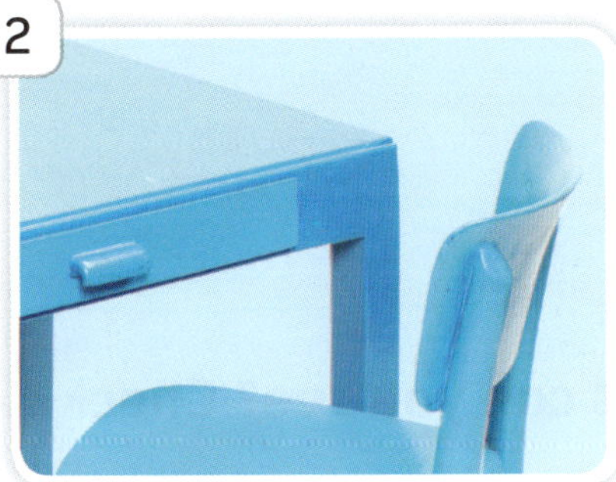

4

Things I learn

1 What's in your school? Say five words.

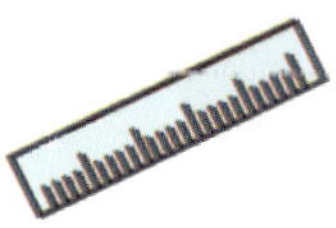

2 My favorite words! Draw and say.

2 Where do we see shapes and colors?

1 Draw.

What do you know?

2 2-1 BBC Watch the video. What colors can you see? Check (✓).

3 2-1 BBC What shapes can you see? Check (✓).

Vocabulary 1

1 Look and count.

2 Match and say.

3 Look and say.

4 Listen and number.

15

My Shapeland

5 Draw and color.

6 Tell a friend about your picture.

Story 1

1 Look and match the shapes.

2 16 Listen and number.

3 Draw three shapes in your neighborhood.

Grammar 1

1 17 Listen and check (✓) or cross (✗).

1

4

2

5

3

6

2 Ask and answer in pairs.

3 Listen and match.

18

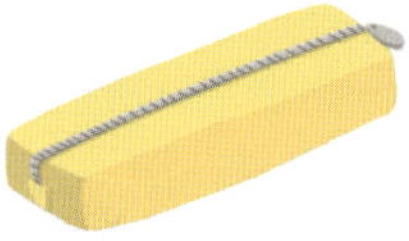
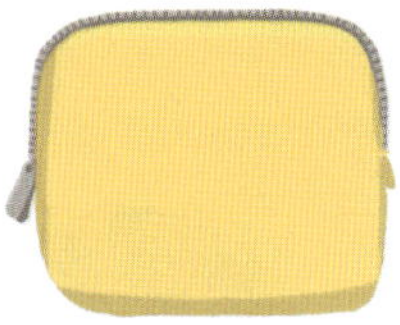

4 Draw and color your school things.

1

3

2

4

5 Tell a friend about your pictures.

Vocabulary 2

1 Look and match.

2 Trace. Then color and say.

3 Listen and number.

19

Vocabulary challenge

4 Listen and check (✓).

20

1

2

3

4

5 Look in your classroom. Draw and color.

Story 2

1 Listen and match.

21

1

2

3

4

a

b

c

d

2 Think and circle. Listen.

22

3 Draw a new kite. Make a wish.

Grammar 2

1 Listen and check (✓).

23

1

2

2 Listen and match.

24

3 Listen and color the stars.

25

4 Talk about the pictures. Use *This* and *That*.

5 Now talk about your classroom. Use *This* and *That*.

Phonics

1 Trace the letters.

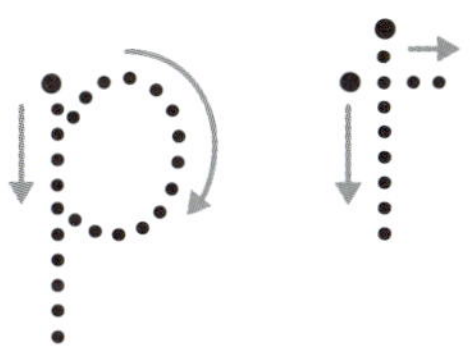

2 Listen, find, and check (✓). 26

p ☑ **t** ☑

3 Look at Activity 2. Find and draw your favorite object beginning with P and then T.

Now I Know

1 What shapes are in your neighborhood? Check (✓) and say.

2 Look and count. Then say.

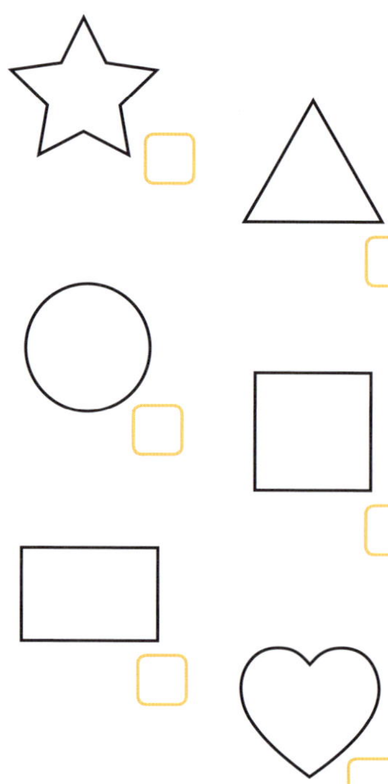

3 Listen and check (✓). 27

4 28 Listen and color.

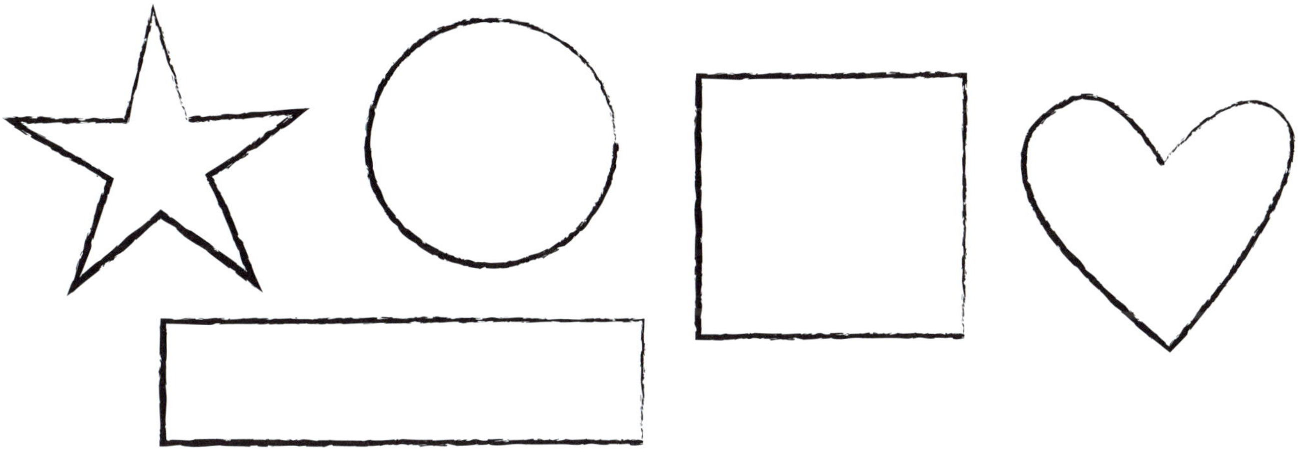

Things I learn

1 Say four shapes and colors.

2 My favorite words! Draw and say.

3 What happens during the day?

1 Draw.

What do you know?

2 Watch the video and number.

3-1

3 Listen and check (✓) or cross (✗).

29

Vocabulary 1

1 Number the pictures. Then say.

2 30 Listen and check (✓).

1

2

3

4

3 Listen and check (✓) or cross (✗) for you.

31

1

2

3

4

5

6

4 Look at Activity 3. Say sentences for you.

Vocabulary challenge

5 Listen. Then say.

32

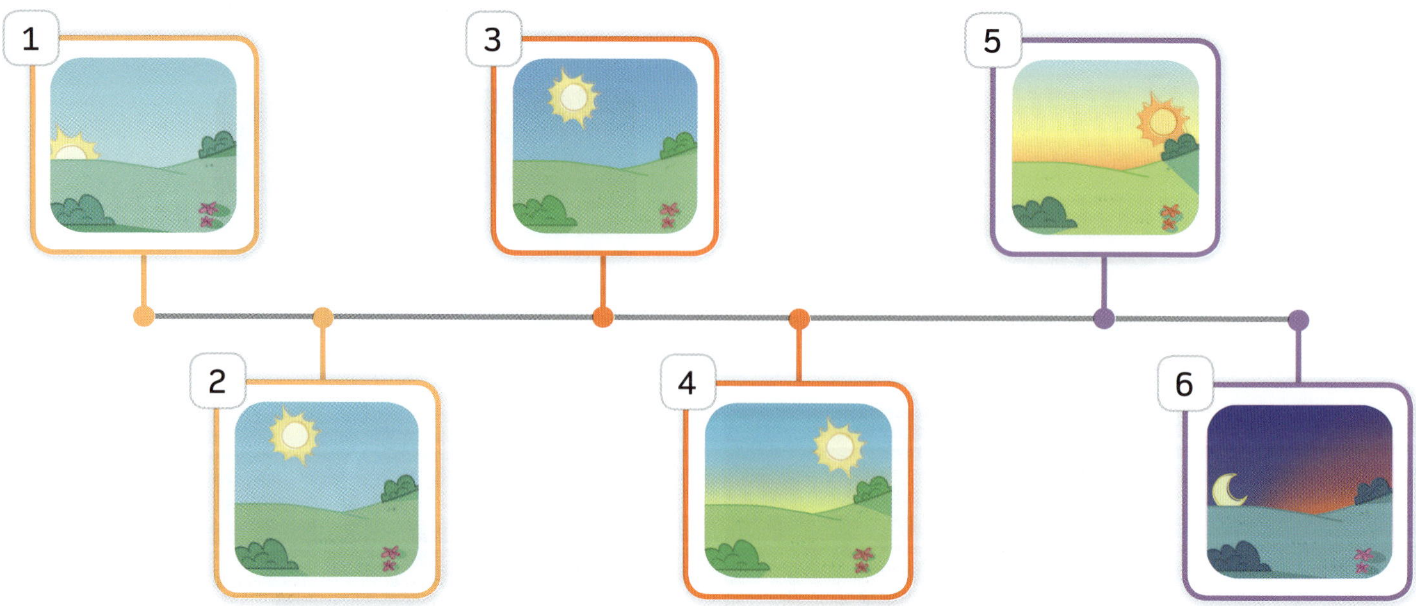

Story 1

1 Listen and check (✓) or cross (✗).

33

1

2

3

4

2 Look and match.

1

2

3

4

a

b

c

d

3 Draw two animals.

Grammar 1

1 Trace and say.

2 Listen and check (✓) or cross (✗).

34

1

3

2

4

3 Ask and answer in pairs.

1

3

5

2

4

6

4 Draw and say.

Vocabulary 2

1 Listen and check (✓).

35

1

2

3

4

2 Match and say for you.

1

2

3

4

5

6

a

b

c

3 36 **Listen and check (✓) or cross (✗). Then circle.**

4 **Look at Activity 3. Say for you. Then tell a friend.**

5 37 **Listen. Check (✓) *do* in green. Check (✓) *go* in red.**

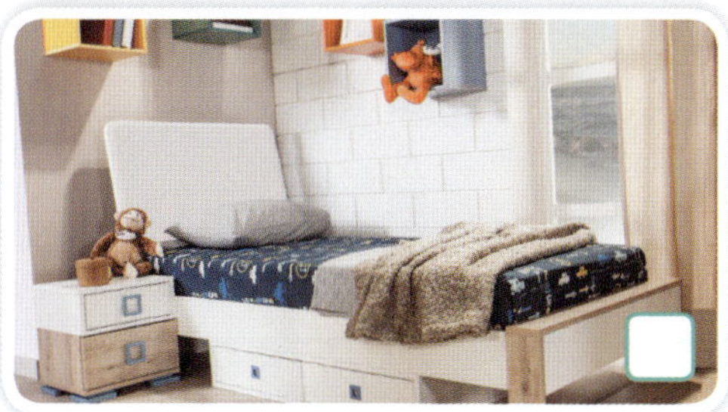

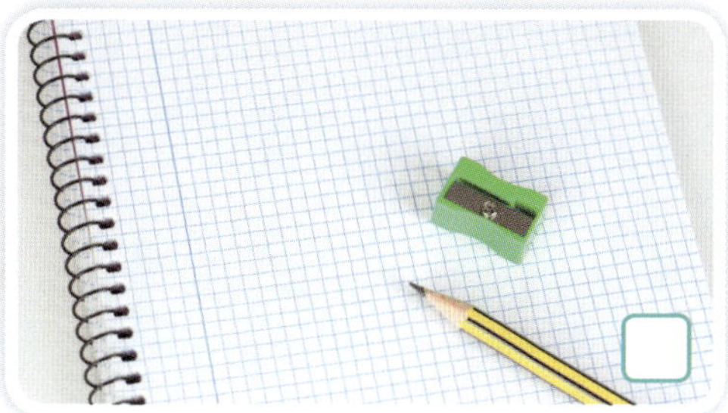

Story 2

1 38 **Number the pictures. Listen to the story again.**

2 **Draw your perfect day. Tell a friend.**

Grammar 2

1 39 **Listen and follow. Then check (✓).**

2 **Match for you. Ask and answer in pairs.**

1

2

3

a

b

c
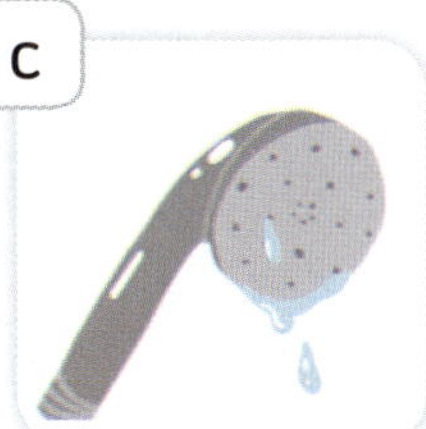

d

e

f

3 Listen and check (✓).

1

4

2

5

3

6

4 Look at Activity 3. Ask a friend.

Phonics

1 Trace the letters.

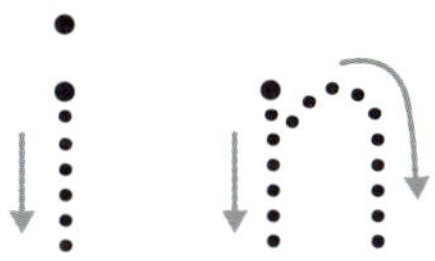

2 41 Listen and check (✓).

i

n

3 Color and find. Then circle the letter.

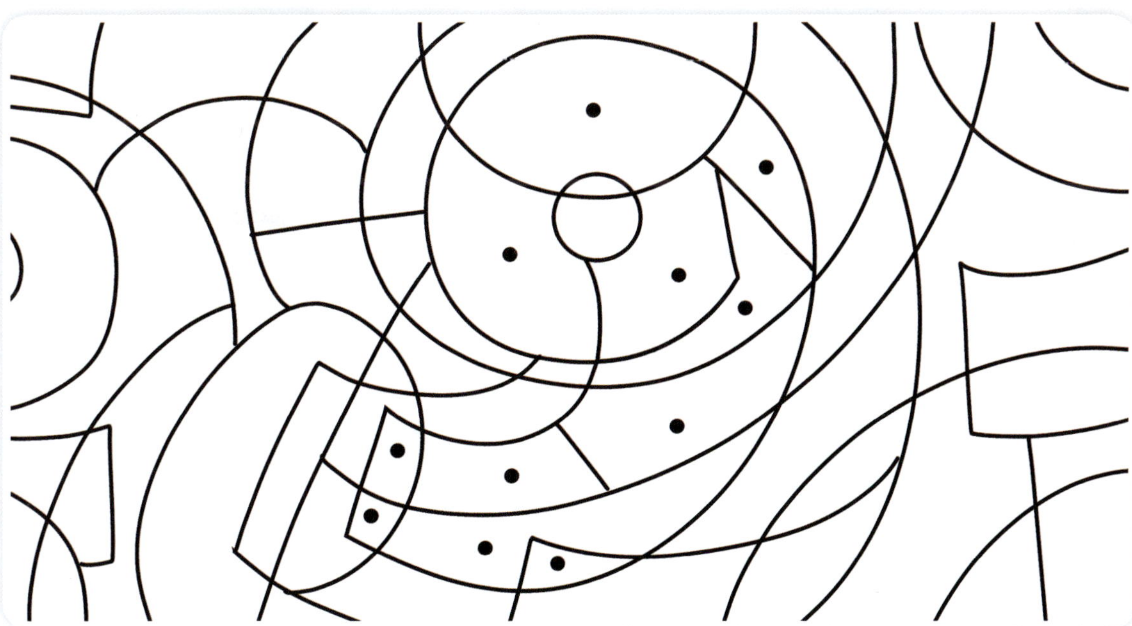

i

n

Now I Know

1 Which word is different? Check (✓).

1

2

3

2 Check (✓) or cross (✗) for you. Do you ... ?

3 Look at Activity 2. Ask a friend.

4 42 **Listen and number. Then ask and answer.**

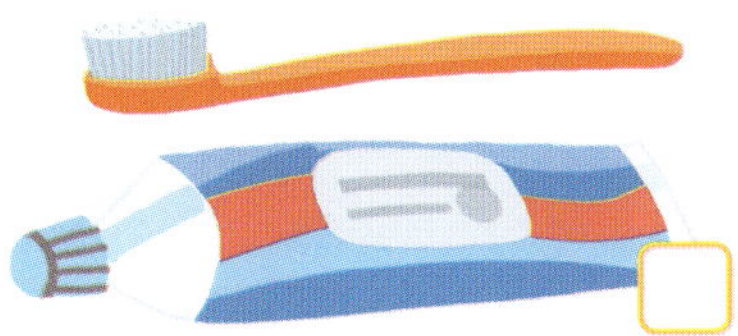

Things I learn

1 **Say four different times of the day.**

2 **Look and say.**

3 **My favorite words! Draw and say.**

4 Why do we have animals?

1 **Draw.**

What do you know?

2 4-1 BBC **Watch the video and number.**

3 4-1 BBC **Where do eggs and milk come from? Check (✓).**

Vocabulary 1

1 Match and say.

1

3

2

4
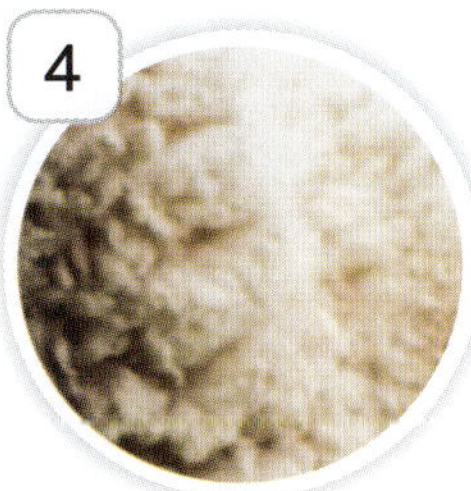

a

goat

c

bee

b

sheep

d

goose

2 Listen and check (✓).

43

1

milk

honey

2

meat

egg

3

4

Vocabulary challenge

3 44 **Listen and number.**

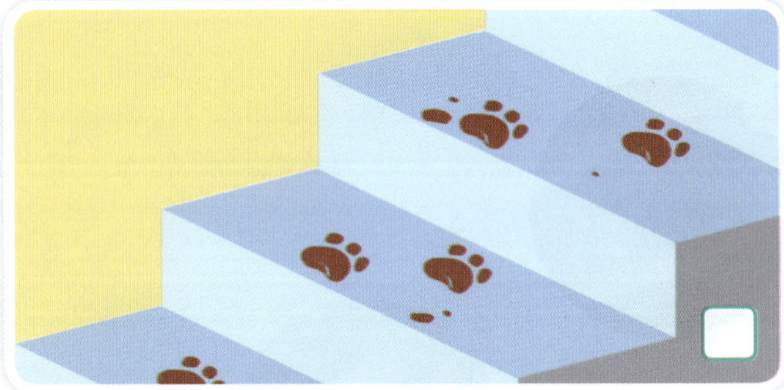

4 **What animals can fly? Check (✓) in red.**

5 **Look at Activity 4. What animals are cute? Circle in green.**

Story 1

1 Trace. Then say.

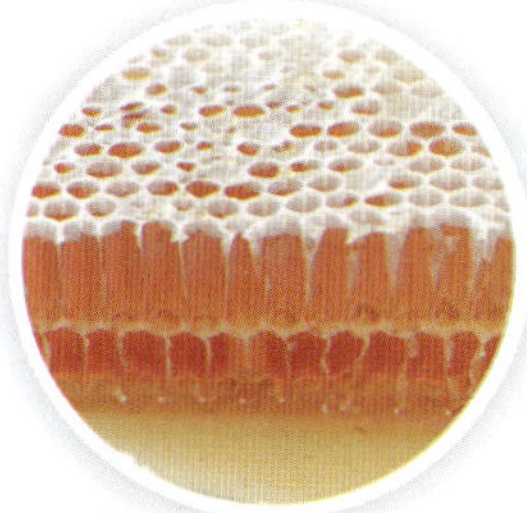

2 Listen and check (✓) or cross (✗).

45

1

2

3

4

Grammar 1

1 46 **Listen and number.**

2 **Look and say. Use *These* and *Those*.**

3 Listen and number.

47

4 Listen and check (✓). Who's speaking?

48

1

2

5 Talk about things in the classroom. Use *These* and *Those*.

Vocabulary 2

1 Match and say.

1

lamb

2

kitten

3

puppy

4

calf

5

kid

6

duckling

a

b

c

d

e

f

2 Find and check (✓). Then say.

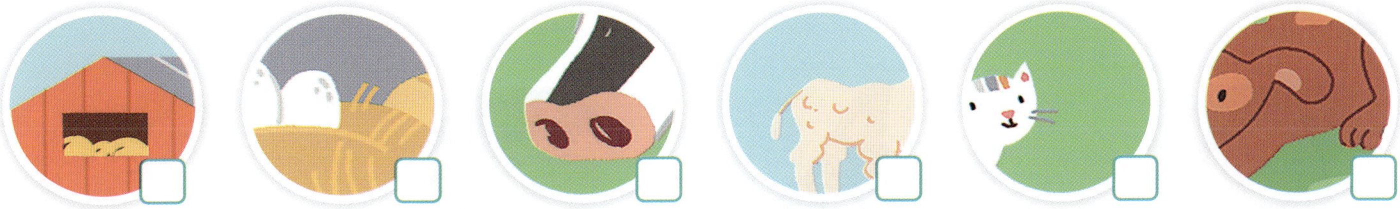

3 Look at Activity 2. Listen and say *Yes* or *No*.

49

4 Listen. Then count and say.

50

Story 2

1 Listen and number. 51

2 Match the animals from the story.

1

2

3

Grammar 2

1 52 **Listen and check (✓).**

1

2

3

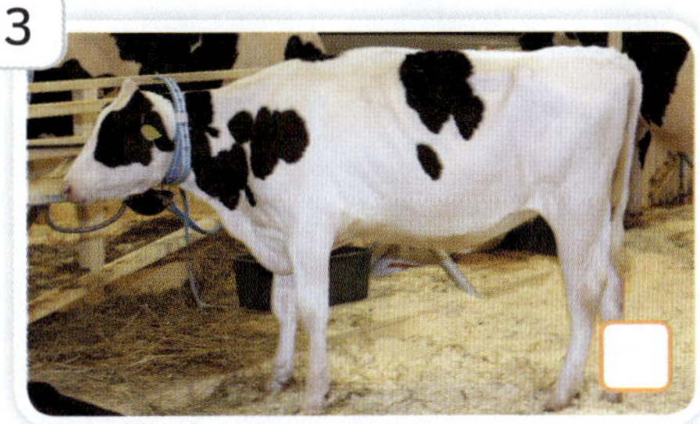

4

2 **Look and say. Use *There is* and *There are*.**

3 Listen and check (✓) or cross (✗).

53

1

4

2

5

3

6

4 Look at Activity 3. Say a correct sentence for each picture.

Phonics

1 Trace the letters.

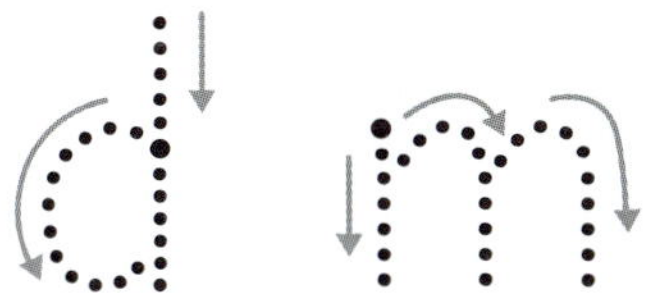

2 54 Find. Then listen and check (✓).

3 Look at the pictures. Say the letters.

Now I Know

1 Look and match. Then say.

2 55 Listen and write the numbers.

3 56 Listen and say *Yes* or *No*.

1

2

3

4

Things I learn

1 Say five different animals on a farm.

2 Look and say.

3 My favorite words! Draw and say.

5 What makes a family?

1 **Draw.**

What do you know?

2 5-1 BBC **Watch the video. Who are they? Say the family words.**

3 5-1 BBC **Watch the video again. Number the people in the correct order.**

Vocabulary 1

1 Read and say the family words.

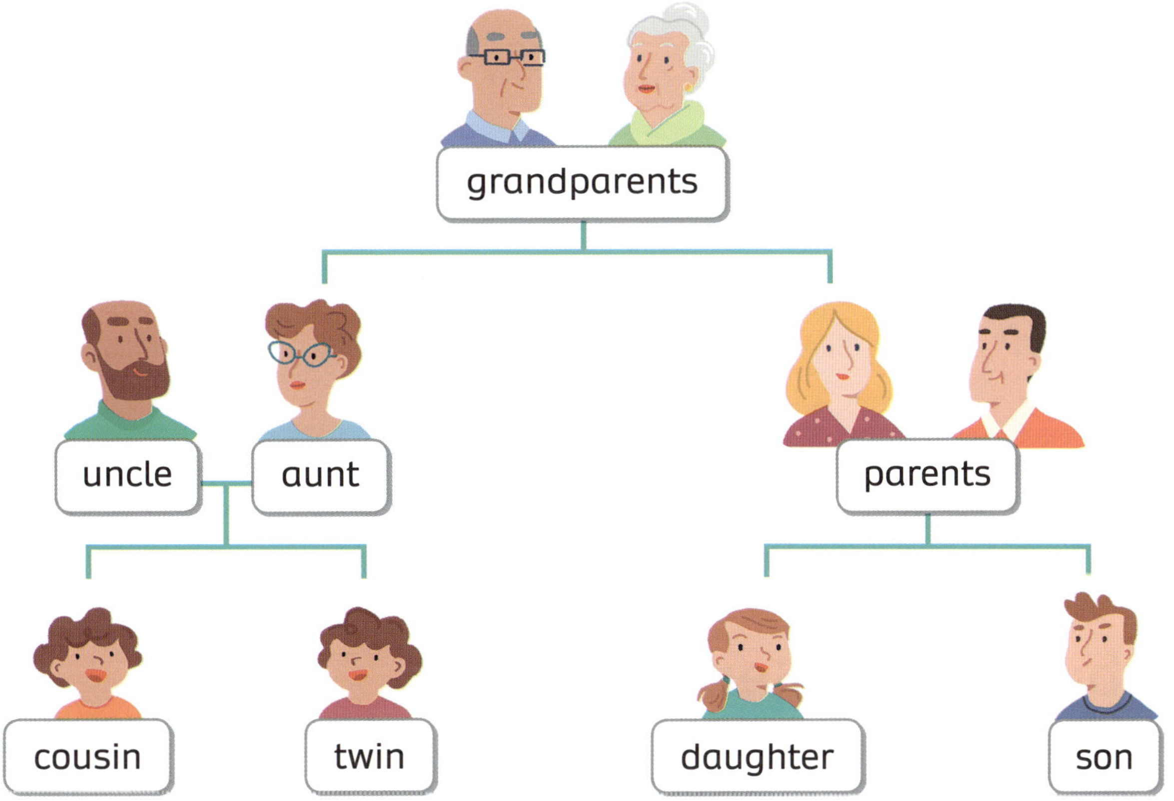

2 Listen and match.

57

1

2

3

4

5

a

b

c

d

e

3 Draw your family tree.

Vocabulary challenge

4 Listen and number. Then say.

58

Story 1

1 Match and say.

1

a

2

b

3

c

4

d

2 Look at Activity 1. Listen and check (✓) or cross (✗).

59

3 Draw a picture of a family. Tell a friend.

Grammar 1

1 Listen and check (✓).

60

2 Listen and check (✓).

61

1

2

3 Listen. Who are they?

62

4 Listen and check (✓) or cross (✗).

63

5 Listen again and answer.

64

6 Look at Activity 4. Ask and answer in pairs.

Vocabulary 2

1 65 **Listen and number. What picture is it?**

live together ☐

talk ☐

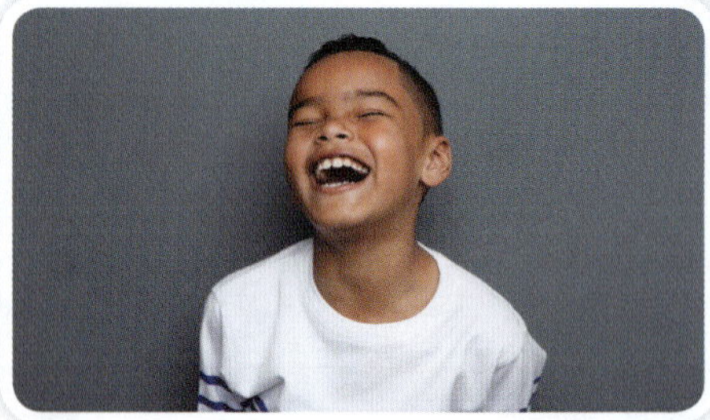

laugh ☐

share ☐

help ☐

old ☐

young ☐

quiet ☐

noisy ☐

2 66 **Listen and check (✓).**

3 Listen and check (✓).

67

1

4

2

5

3

6

4 Draw. How do you help your family?

Story 2

1 Listen and number.

68

2 What's the message of the story? Check (✓).

3 Draw. How do you work hard? How do you play?

Grammar 2

1 Listen. Say the correct word.

69

1

3

2

4

2 Listen to the rhyme. Number the pictures.

70

☐

☐

☐

☐

3 Look at Activity 2. Can you say the rhyme?

4 Listen and check (✓) or cross (✗).

71

1 

4 

2 

5 

3 

6 

5 Listen and check (✓) or cross (✗) for you.

72

Name						

6 Now ask two friends.

Phonics

1 Trace the letters.

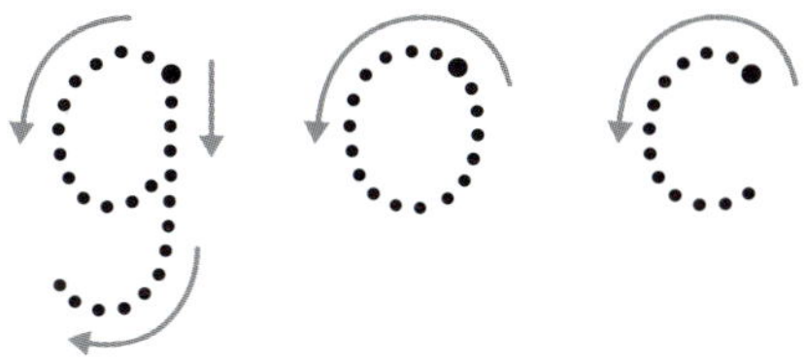

2 73 Find. Then listen and check (✓). Check the g words in green. Check the c words in red.

3 Look at Activity 2. Find and say.

Now I Know

1 Check (✓) the odd one out.

1

2

3

4

2 74 Listen and say the words.

3 Talk about the picture. Use family words.

4 Listen and number. Then ask and answer in pairs.

75

Things I learn

1 Say five family words.

2 Look and say.

3 My favorite words! Draw and say.

6 How are we the same and different?

1 Draw.

What do you know?

2 6-1 BBC Watch the video and number.

3 What's your favorite music and dance? Talk in pairs.

Vocabulary 1

1 **Match and say.**

2 76 **Listen and check (✓).**

1

2

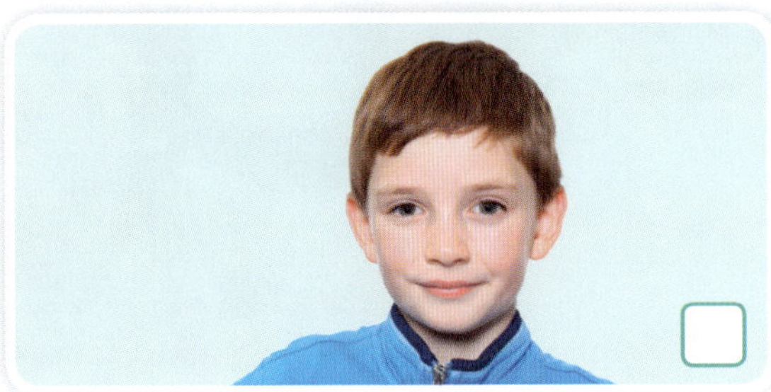

3 Listen. Draw and color.

77

1

2

Vocabulary challenge

4 Listen and number.

78

5 Think about your friends. Check (✓) and say.

Story 1

1 79 **Listen and check (✓) or cross (✗).**

1

3

5

2

4

6

2 **Circle. How are they the same? How are they different?**

3 **What's the message of the story? Draw.**

Grammar 1

1 80 **Listen and color.**

1 2 3 4 5 6

2 **Draw and color the monsters. Tell a friend.**

3 **Describe yourself and your mom or dad.**

4 Listen and check (✓) or cross (✗).

81

1 ☐ 2 ☐ 3 ☐ 4 ☐ 5 ☐ 6 ☐

5 Listen and check (✓).

82

1

2

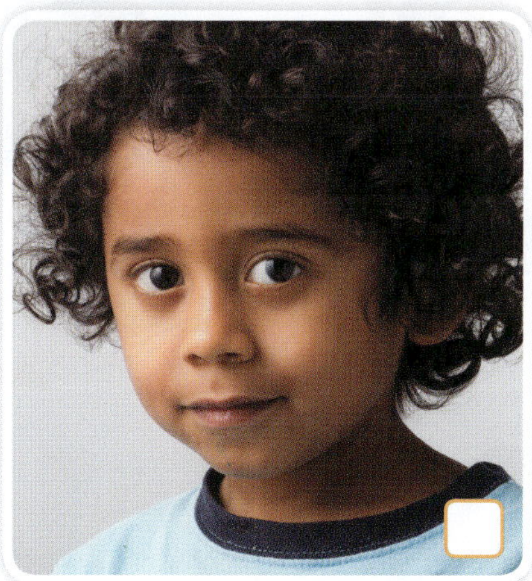

6 Look at Activity 5. Ask and answer in pairs.

Vocabulary 2

1 Match and say.

1 2 3 4 5 6

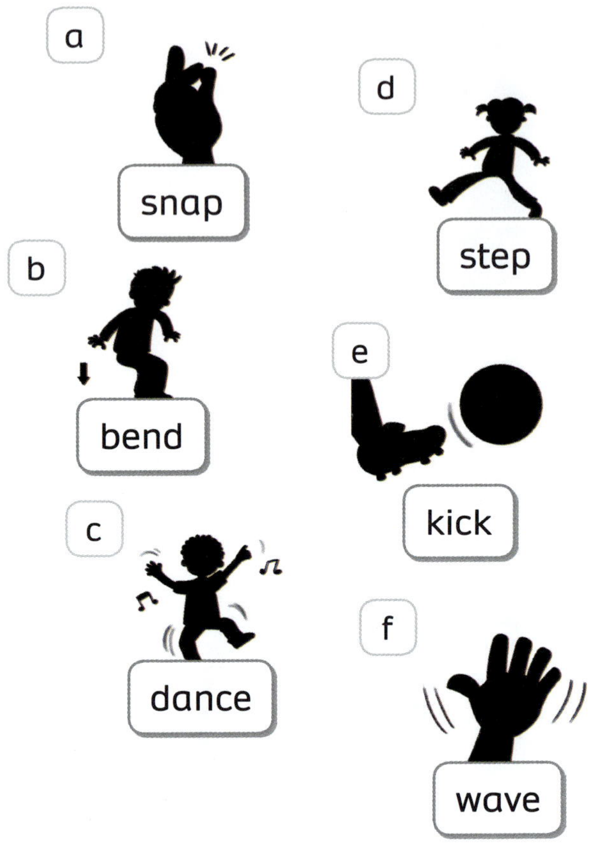

a snap
b bend
c dance
d step
e kick
f wave

2 Listen and check (✓) the actions you hear.

83

3 Listen and check (✓) or cross (✗).

84

1

3

2

4

4 Check (✓) the describing words.

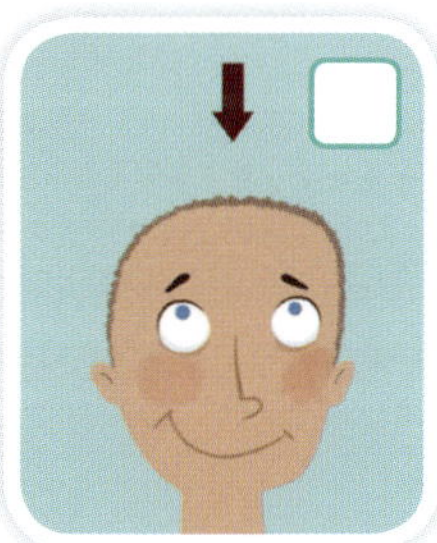

5 Listen and say the describing words you hear.

85

Story 2

1 Match and say.

a 

1 

d 

b 

2 

e 

c 

3 

f 

2 Listen and check (✓) the musical instruments you hear.

86

3 Draw a dance from your country or region.

Grammar 2

1 Listen and check (✓).

87

1

3

2

4

2 Listen and say the opposite.

88

3 Look and say.

1

3

5

2

4

6

4 Listen and number. 89

5 Look and say.

1

3

2

4

6 Talk in pairs about your things.

Phonics

1 Trace the letters.

c k c k

2 90 Check (✓) the odd one out. Then listen.

1

2

3

3 Color and find. Then match.

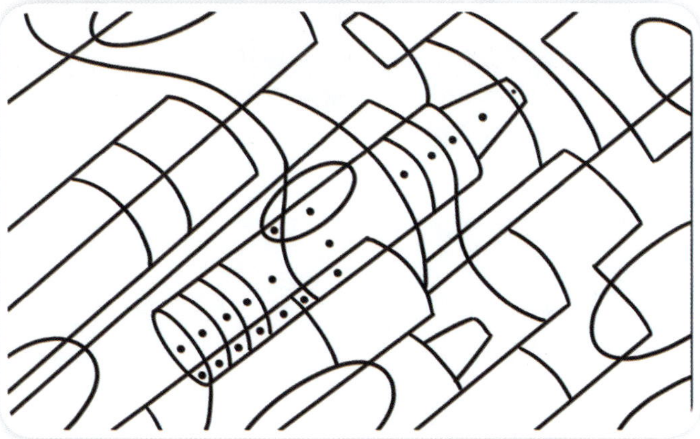

c k

Now I Know

1 91 **Listen and check (✓) or cross (✗).**

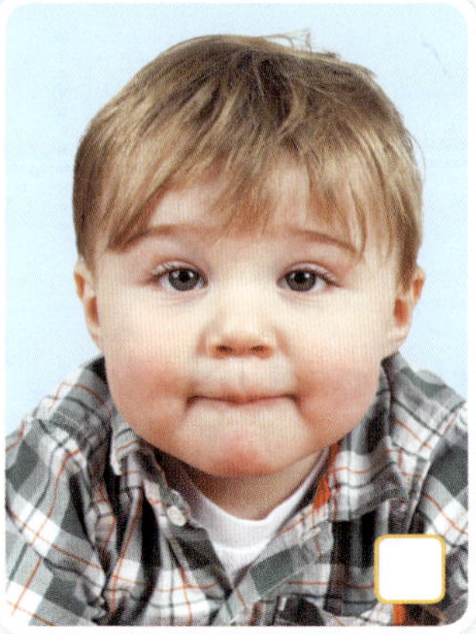
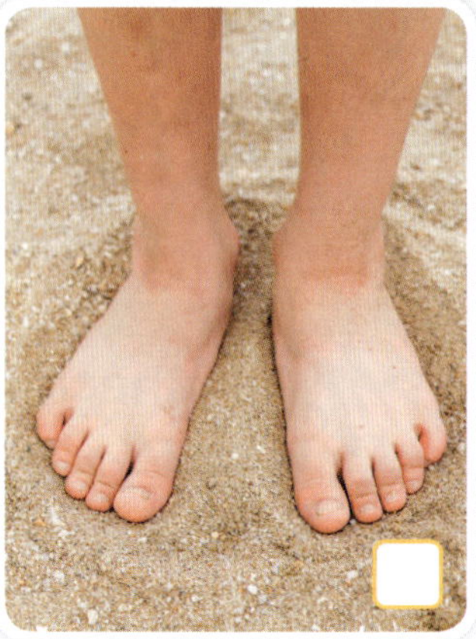

2 **Say the action words.**

1
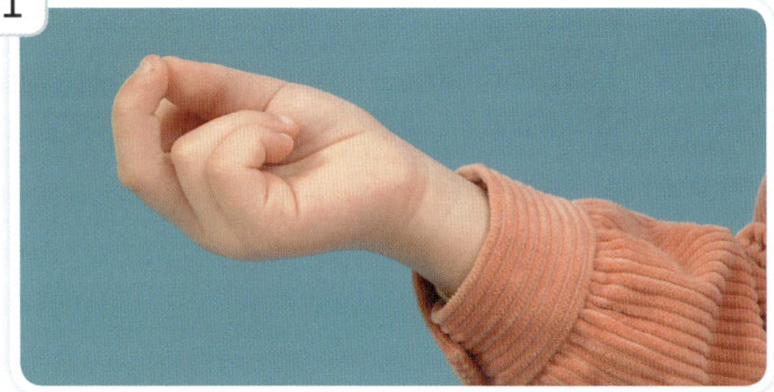

4

2

5

3

6

3 Listen and answer.

92

1 ☐
2 ☐
3 ☐
4 ☐

Things I learn

1 Say five words to describe people.

2 Look and say.

3 My favorite words! Draw and say.

7 Why do we do hobbies?

1 Draw.

What do you know?

2 7-1 BBC Watch the video and number.

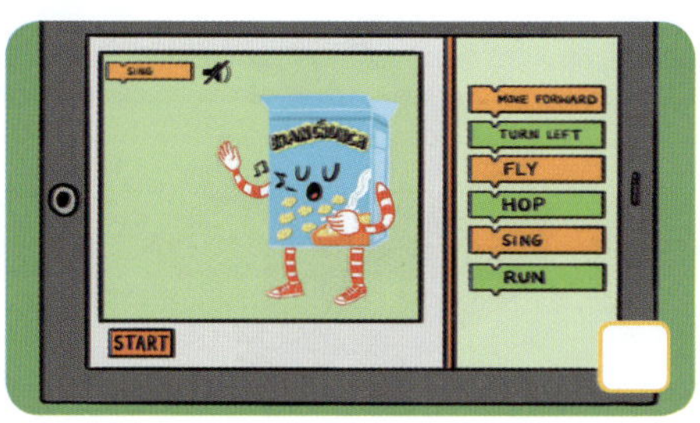

3 What can you do? Check (✓).

Vocabulary 1

1 Find and circle.

~~climb~~ code hop ride skip swim type

G	U	O	R	P	S	K	T	Y	P	E
K	S	W	I	M	K	C	L	I	M	B
W	C	O	D	E	I	O	E	Z	X	U
G	L	B	E	A	P	N	H	O	P	I
O	D	C	L	F	I	T	R	E	A	N

2 Look and write.

code hop ~~ride~~ skip swim type

1

r i d e a bike

3

c ___ ___ ___

5

s ___ ___ ___

2

t ___ ___ ___

4

___ w ___ ___

6

h ___ ___

3 Listen and match.

93

1

2

3

4 Listen and trace.

94

I go to the zoo.

I'm at the park.

1

2

5 Draw for you. Then say.

Story 1

1 Listen and circle T (true) or F (false).

95

1	T	F	4	T	F
2	T	F	5	T	F
3	T	F	6	T	F

2 Match the words that rhyme. Then listen.

96

1 

3 

2 

4 

a 

c 

d 

b 

3 Think and draw.

Grammar 1

I **can** swim.	**Can** you swim?
I **can't** swim.	**Yes**, I **can**. / **No**, I **can't**.

1 Listen and number. Then say.

97

	hop	swim	climb	ride a bike	type fast	sing	dance
 Alex ☐	✓	✗	✓	✗	✓	✗	✓
 Aisha ☐	✓	✓	✓	✓	✗	✓	✓
 Emma ☐	✗	✓	✗	✓	✓	✓	✓

2 Look at Activity 1. Listen and check (✓) or cross (✗).

98

3 Look at Activity 1. Ask and answer in pairs.

4 Check (✓) or cross (✗) for you. Tell a friend.

5 Look at the pictures. Ask a friend.

6 Draw. What can you do? What can't you do?

✓

✗

Vocabulary 2

1 Listen and number.

99

2 Read and match.

1

2

3

4

board game
computer
game
hobby
phone
screen
soccer
sports

5

6

7

8

3 Circle five words. Then write.

1 p _ _ _ _
2 s _ _ _ _ _
3 c _ _ _ _ _ _ _
4 g _ _ _
5 h _ _ _ _

4 Listen and check (✓).

100

1

a ☐ b ☐ c ☐

3

a ☐ b ☐ c ☐

2

a ☐ b ☐ c ☐

4

a ☐ b ☐ c ☐

Vocabulary challenge

5 Listen and number.

101

runner ☐

swimmer ☐

athlete ☐

player ☐

Story 2

1 Listen and check (✓).

102

1

2

2 Listen and check (✓) or cross (✗).

103

1 ☐
2 ☐
3 ☐
4 ☐
5 ☐
6 ☐

3 Draw your favorite Olympic and Paralympic sport.

Grammar 2

1 Trace and match. Then say.

I	him
you	them
he	you
she	us
we	me
they	her

2 Listen and match.

104

1

3

a

c

2

4

b

d

3 Listen and say.

105

4 Listen and number.

106

a

c

e

b

d

f

5 Look at Activity 4. Talk in pairs.

Phonics

1 Trace the letters.

r u b

2 Say and match.

r

u

b

3 Color and find. Then write the letters.

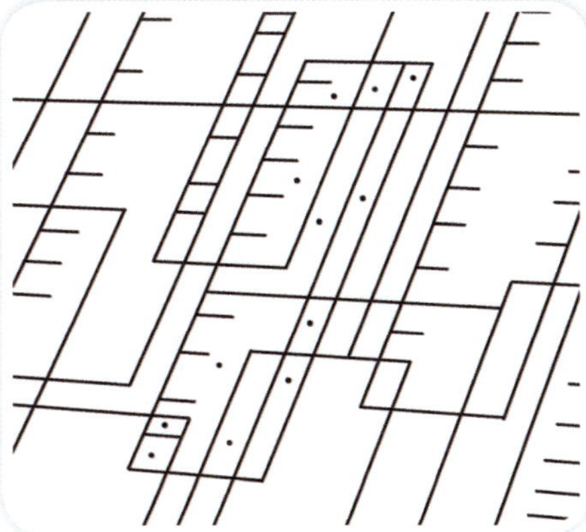

Now I Know

1 Read and sort.

board game ~~climb~~ code
computer game hop
~~phone~~ ride a bike screen
swim type

Actions	Things
climb	phone

2 Listen and check (✓).

107

1

2

3

4

3 Check (✓) or cross (✗) for you. Talk in pairs.

4 Look and say.

1 
2 
3 
4 

Things I learn

1 Say five hobby words.

swim

2 Say and write.

....

3 My favorite words! Draw and say.

....

....

....

8 What food do we eat?

1 Draw or write.

What do you know?

2 What do you learn about in this unit? Circle.

Art

Food

Hobbies

3 ▶ 8-1 BBC Watch the video. Check (✓) the fruits you see.

4 ▶ 8-1 BBC 108 Watch the video again. Then listen and circle T (true) or F (false).

1 T F

2 T F

3 T F

4 T F

5 T F

Vocabulary 1

1 Look and circle.

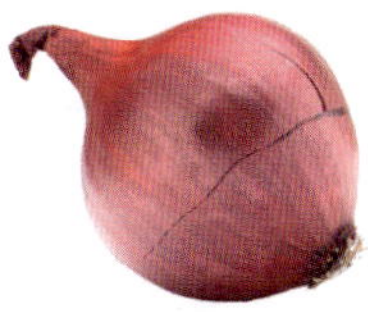

1 lemon / onion

3 lemon / pear

5 grapes / peas

7 pineapple / onion

2 potato / carrot

4 pineapple / carrot

6 onion / grapes

8 potato / pear

2 Order the letters. Write the words.

1  a / p / e / s

....

2  r / e / a / p

....

3  s / p / a / g / e / r

....

4  n / o / o / n / i

....

5  t / r / a / c / o / r

....

6  m / o / l / e / n

....

7  t / o / p / o / a / t

....

8  p / l / e / p / n / e / p / i / a

....

3 Complete the crossword.

Across

1

5

6

7
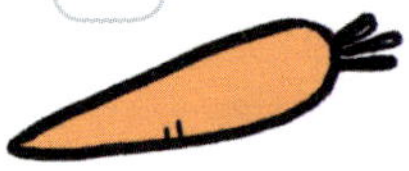

8

Down

2

3

4

4 Listen and number.

109

5 Read. Circle the color words. Underline the food words.

a red onion   a green apple

6 Draw and color. Then write.

Story 1

1 110 Listen and check (✓) or cross (✗).

1

2

3

4

5

2 111 Listen and number.

3 Think and draw.

Grammar 1

I **like** bananas.
I **don't like** oranges.

Do you **like** bananas?
Yes, I **do**. / **No**, I **don't**.

1 Listen and check (✓).

112

2 Look and say for Hassid.

✓

✗

✗

✓

✓

✗

3 Check (✓) or cross (✗) for you. Tell a friend.

grapes ☐

onions ☐

peas ☐

pears ☐

4 Look at the pictures. Ask and answer in pairs.

1

pineapples ?

2

lemons ?

3

carrots ?

4

potatoes ?

5 What do you like? What don't you like? Draw.

Vocabulary 2

1 Find and circle. Then write.

y __ __ __ __ __
s __ __ __
b __ __ __ __
r __ __ __
b __ __ __ __
p __ __ __ __
c __ __ __ __ __
l __ __ __

2 Look and check (✓) or cross (✗).

1 cookie ☐

3 lime ☐

5 rice ☐

7 soup ☐

2 bread ☐

4 yogurt ☐

6 pasta ☐

8 cookie ☐

3 Listen. Match the foods from the *Eat Well* plate.

113

4 Listen and circle *yes* or *no*.

114

1	yes	no	4	yes	no	6	yes	no
2	yes	no	5	yes	no	7	yes	no
3	yes	no						

Vocabulary challenge

5 Listen and number.

115

6 Read and draw. Then say.

slice

bowl

plate

Story 2

1 Look and match.

a 

b 

c 

d 

e 

f 

2 Listen and check (✓).

116

1  ☐  ☐

2  ☐ 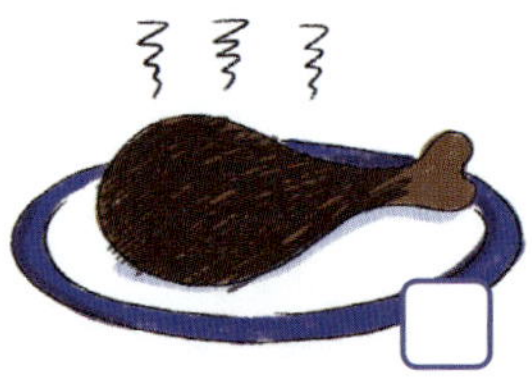 ☐

3  ☐  ☐

4  ☐  ☐

3 What's the story about? Draw.

Grammar 2

He like**s** blue peas.	She **doesn't** like blue peas.
Does he like blue peas?	Yes, he **does**.
Does she like blue peas?	No, she **doesn't**.

1 Listen and check (✓).

117

1

3

2

4

2 Listen and check (✓) or cross (✗).

118

1 		
2 		
3 		

3 Look and say.

	beans	yogurt	soup	cookies
 Amy	☹	🙂	☹	🙂
 Tom	🙂	☹	🙂	🙂

4 Listen. Check (✓) and answer.

119

1	🙂	☐	☹	☐	4	🙂	☐	☹	☐
2	🙂	☐	☹	☐	5	🙂	☐	☹	☐
3	🙂	☐	☹	☐	6	🙂	☐	☹	☐

5 Listen and answer for you.

120

1

2

3

4

5

6

Phonics

1 Trace the letters.

f l l l

2 121 Listen and point. Then check (✓) in blue for *f* and in green for *l*.

f ☑ l ☑

3 122 Listen and check (✓) the odd one out.

 ☐  ☐ 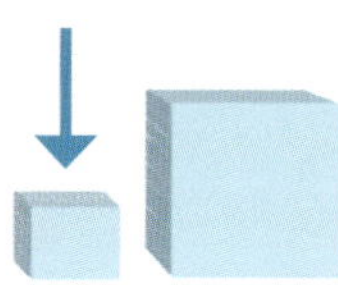 ☐  ☐  ☐  ☐

4 Draw and say.

f	l	ll

Now I Know

1 Circle the odd one out.

1

pear

grape

onion

lime

2

pineapple

carrot

potato

peas

3

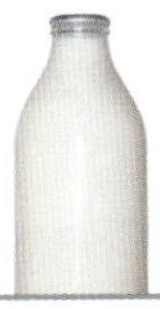
milk

yogurt

bread

cheese

2 Look at Activity 1. Write the words.

1

potato, carrot, ...

3

rice, pasta, ...

2

pear, lime, ...

4

cheese, ...

3 123 Listen and draw.

1

2

3

4

Things I learn

1 Look and say the food words.

2 Write three food words.

....

3 My favorite words! Draw and write.

....

9 How do we play?

1 Draw or write.

What do you know?

2 What do you learn about in this unit? Circle.

Friends Toys Food

3 How many? Write the numbers. Then watch the video.

9-1 BBC

.... teddy bear
.... cars
.... dolls
.... robots

4 Make your own bar chart. Draw the toys.

4 balls 3 kites 1 robot 2 teddy bears

4
3
2
1

....

Vocabulary 1

1 Write the missing letters.

1 bl ___ cks

2 h ___ l ___ - h ___ ___ p

3 sc ___ ___ t ___ r

4 t ___ y b ___ ___ t

5 s ___ u ___ f ___ ___ a ___ i ___ al

6 r ___ b ___ t

7 t ___ y tr ___ ck

8 ___ ct ___ ___ n f ___ g ___ r ___

2 Look at Activity 1. Read and match.

1 It's yellow.
2 It's blue and white.
3 It's red and round.
4 It's gray. It has red feet.
5 It's brown. It has big eyes.
6 It has two wheels.

a hula-hoop
b scooter
c robot
d action figure
e toy boat
f stuffed animal

3 Listen. Then choose and write.

124

blocks   hula-hoop   stuffed animal   ~~truck~~

1 My toy ......truck...... is yellow.

2 I have my .... in a box.

3 I have a .... on my bed.

4 My .... is round and purple.

4 Write the alphabet.

Z C F R H E V N W P J T X

A B __ D __ __ G __ I __ K L M __ O __ Q __ S __ U __ __ __ Y __

5 Write the words in alphabetical order.

1

car
box
doll
action figure

....
....
....
....

2

box
blocks
truck
bed

....
....
....
....

Story 1

1 Listen and check (✓). Who says it?

125

1

3

2

4

2 Listen and point. Say the names.

126

3 Think and draw. What do you share?

Grammar 1

Whose ball is this?  It's Tommy**'s** ball.

1 Listen and match.

127

Sally

Oliver

Ben

2 Read and circle.

1 It's **Aimee / Aimee's** bike.

2 This is **Mark's / Marks** toy boat.

3 It's **Stanley / Stanley's** hula-hoop.

4 This is the **boy / boy's** toy truck.

3 Look and write.

1 Whose scooter is it?
It's Marina's scooter.

Marina

2 Whose ball is it?
It's .... ball.

Fernando

3 .... block is it?
It's .... block.

Lidia

4 .... hula-hoop is it?
It's .... hula-hoop.

Ali

4 Write the words in order.

1 Anita's / action figure / It's
It's Anita's action figure .

2 toy truck / It's / David's
....

3 Sam's / It's / robot
....

4 it / Whose / is / bike
.... ?

Vocabulary 2

1 Order the letters. Write the words.

1 s / h / o / c / c / p / o / t / h

hopscotch

2 k / a / t / e u / r / n / s / t

3 k / o / n / e / m / y r / a / b / s

4 g / i / n / s / w / s

5 i / l / d / e / s

6 a / g / t

7 s / o / l / e

8 n / i / w

2 128 Listen and say. Then check (✓).

1

2

3

3 Look at Activity 1. Read and write the numbers.

She's on the monkey bars. ....

He's on the slide. ....

They're playing hopscotch. ....

They're playing tag. ....

Vocabulary challenge

4 Look at the examples and write.

This is a slide. I slide down. This is a swing. I can swing.

1 It's a .... !

3 Let's .... down!

2 It's a ....

4 This girl can ....

Story 2

1 129 **Listen and number.**

2 130 **Listen and circle T (true) or F (false).**

1 T F
2 T F
3 T F
4 T F
5 T F
6 T F
7 T F
8 T F
9 T F

3 **Draw a game you play.**

Grammar 2

1 Read and match.

my	hers
your	theirs
his	mine
her	his
our	yours
their	ours

2 Listen and number.

131

3 Look at Activity 2. Ask and answer.

Is this my book?

Yes, this book is yours.

4 Read and match.

1 This is **my** hula-hoop.

2 This is **their** toy truck.

3 This is **his** toy boat.

4 They're **your** blocks.

a It's **his**.

b They're **yours**.

c It's **theirs**.

d It's **mine**.

5 Choose and write.

his **mine** **ours**

This hula-hoop is
....

This scooter is
....

These blocks are
....

6 Draw and write for you and your friend.

....

....

Phonics

1 Trace the letters.

j g h

2 Listen and circle.

132

1 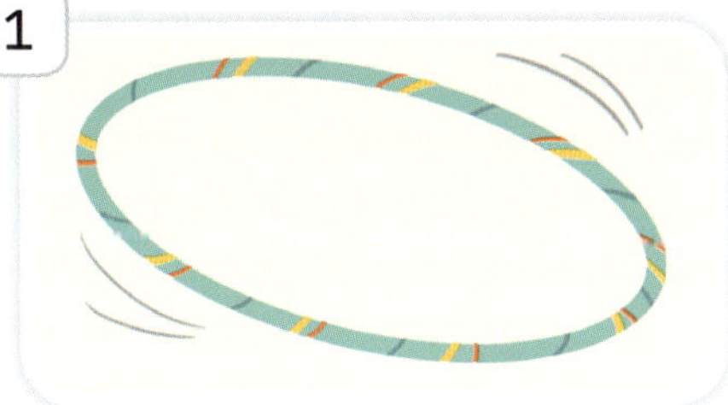

h j

3 

j g

5 

j h

2 

h j

4 

h g

6 

h j

3 Listen and number. Then say.

133

Now I Know

1 Read and sort.

action figure   blocks   hopscotch   hula-hoop   lose
monkey bars   slide   stuffed animal   swings   tag
take turns   toy boat   toy truck   win

Games	Toys	Things on a playground

2 Listen and match. Then write.

134

Zehra   Melisa   Aydin   Esma

1 ......Whose...... blocks are they?
They're ......Esma's...... blocks.

2 .... action figure is it?
It's .... action figure.

3 .... stuffed animal is it?
It's .... stuffed animal.

4 .... hula-hoop is it?
It's .... hula-hoop.

3 Choose and write.

his ~~mine~~ ours theirs yours

1 This is **my** toy truck. It's mine .
2 This is **your** doll. It's ....
3 This is **Ben's** scooter. It's ....
4 These are **our** blocks. They're ....
5 These are **their** toys. They're ....

Things I learn

1 How do you play? Write.

How I play alone	How I play with my friends
I play with my action figure .	We play a skipping game .
I play with my	We play ....
I play with my	We play ....

2 My new words! Draw and write.

....

3 My favorite words in this unit! Write.

....

10 What clothes do we wear?

1 Draw or write.

What do you know?

2 What do you learn about in this unit? Circle and write.

Sports Food Clothes wear go take

.... we ....

3 10-1 BBC What clothes do you hear? Watch the video and circle.

dress jeans shirt
shoes skirt
socks T-shirt

4 What clothes are good for sports? Check (✓).

 ☐

 ☐

 ☐

 ☐

 ☐

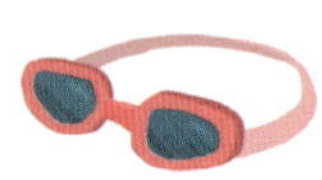 ☐

Vocabulary 1

1 Write the missing letters.

1 b o o t s 2 s _ _ _ _ _ _ 3 j _ _ _ _ _

4 s _ _ _ _ _ 5 g _ _ _ _ _ 6 s _ _ _ _ _ _

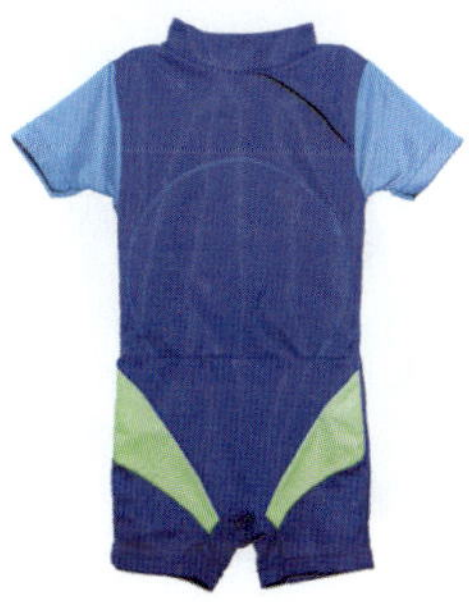

7 b _ _ _ _ _ _ s _ _ _ 8 b _ _ _ _ _

2 Look at Activity 1. Read and circle.

1 You wear it for swimming. **blouse / bathing suit**

2 You wear them on your hands. **gloves / sandals**

3 You wear them for soccer. **boots / sweater**

4 You wear it when it's cold. **shorts / jacket**

3 What clothes do you have? Check (✓) and write.

	I have ...	How many?	What color?
bathing suit	☐		
boots	☐		
gloves	☐		
blouse	☐		
sandals	☐		
jacket	☐		
shorts	☐		
sweater	☐		

4 Listen and number.

135

a

☐

b

☐

c

☐

d

☐

e

☐

5 Read and match.

1	bathing	a	boots
2	dancing	b	goggles
3	horseback-riding	c	helmet
4	soccer	d	shoes
5	swimming	e	suit

Story 1

1 Match and say.

1

2

3

2 Listen and say. Then check (✓).

136

1

2

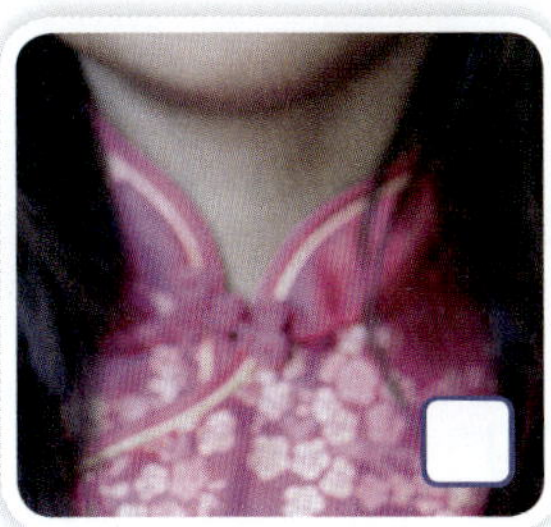

3

4

3 Think and draw clothes.

wool	silk	cotton

Grammar 1

I**'m wearing** a T-shirt. You**'re wearing** a T-shirt. He**'s wearing** a T-shirt.	I**'m not wearing** a blouse. You **aren't wearing** a blouse. She **isn't wearing** a blouse.

1 Read and circle T (true) or F (false).

Marc

Megan

1 Marc's wearing a bathing suit. T F

2 He's wearing boots. T F

3 Marc isn't wearing a sweater. T F

4 Megan's wearing a T-shirt. T F

5 She isn't wearing gloves. T F

6 Megan isn't wearing sandals. T F

2 Look, read, and circle.

I'm / I'm not wearing a sweater.
I'm / I'm not wearing shorts.

You're / You aren't wearing a jacket.
You're / You aren't wearing a T-shirt.

She's / She isn't wearing boots.
She's / She isn't wearing sandals.

3 Draw and write about you.

I'm ....
....
I'm not ....
....

4 Write about your friend.

My friend .... wearing ....
He/She .... wearing ....

Vocabulary 2

1 Look and write the missing letters.

1 __ a __ __

3 __ __ i __ __

5 __ oo __

7 __ __ i __

2 __ a __ __

4 __ __ o __ __

6 __ e __

8 __ __ y

2 Choose and write.

book cotton girl ~~socks~~ sweater

1 wet ......socks......
2 cool ....
3 warm ....
4 tall ....
5 thin ....

3 Look at Activity 1. Read and write.

1 My T-shirt isn't wet. It's ......dry...... .
2 My mom isn't tall. She's ....
3 This book isn't thin. It's ....
4 It's hot today. I'm wearing a .... cotton shirt.
5 It's cold today. I'm wearing a .... sweater.

4 Look at the picture. Read and write the numbers.

It's wet. ....

It's dry. ....

She's tall. ....

He has a thin book. ....

Vocabulary challenge

5 Look, choose, and write.

button pocket sleeve zipper

1 ....

2 ....

3 ....

4 ....

6 Look and answer.

The jacket has …

.... sleeves.

.... buttons.

.... zippers.

.... pockets.

Story 2

1 Listen and circle T (true) or F (false).

137

1	T	F	4	T	F
2	T	F	5	T	F
3	T	F	6	T	F

2 Listen and say. Then number.

138

3 Draw a uniform you like.

Grammar 2

Are you **wearing** a dress? **Yes**, I **am**. / **No**, I**'m not**.

Is he/she **wearing** a T-shirt? **Yes**, he/she **is**. / **No**, he/she **isn't**.

1 Listen and number.

139

2 Circle the answers for you.

1 Are you wearing a bathing suit?

Yes, I am. / No, I'm not.

2 Is your teacher wearing boots?

Yes, he / she is.

No, he / she isn't.

3 Are you wearing warm clothes?

Yes, I am. / No, I'm not.

4 Is your friend wearing a blouse?

Yes, he / she is.

No, he / she isn't.

3 Write the words in order. Make questions.

1 you / gloves / wearing / Are

Are you wearing gloves ?

2 jacket / wearing / Is / a / Sunita

.... ?

3 wearing / you / Are / sandals

.... ?

4 Matias / bathing suit / a / wearing / Is

.... ?

5 a / Is / blouse / Sunita / wearing

.... ?

4 Look and write answers to Activity 3.

Me	✓	✓	✗	✗	✗	✗
Sunita	✗	✗	✗	✓	✓	✓
Matias	✓	✓	✗	✗	✗	✗

1 No, I'm not .

2 No, ...

3 ....

4 ....

5 ....

5 Look at Activity 4. Ask and answer in pairs.

Is Matias wearing a sweater?

Yes, he is.

Phonics

1 Trace the letters.

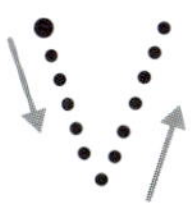

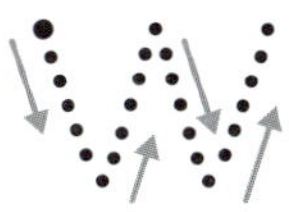

2 Look and say. Check (✓) the /v/ and the /w/ words.

v

w

3 140 Listen and say. Then circle the letter.

w b v

u w v

Now I Know

1 Find and circle seven clothes words.

2 Look at Activity 1. Write the words.

1 ....

2 ....

3 ....

4 ....

5 ....

6 ....

7 ....

3 Look at Activity 2. Listen and say the words.

141

4 Write the opposites.

1 It isn't dry. It's _ _ _ .

2 It isn't warm. It's _ _ _ _ .

3 It isn't thin. It's _ _ _ _ _ .

4 It isn't short. It's _ _ _ _ .

5 Read, choose, and write.

~~'m~~ 'm not wearing

WHAT AM I WEARING?

I'm Carlos.

I *'m* .... wearing a shirt.

I'm .... wearing a sweater.

I .... wearing shorts and sandals.

I'm not .... boots.

6 Complete the questions. Then ask and answer.

.... he wearing a jacket?

No, he ....

.... he wearing a shirt?

Yes, he ....

Things I learn

1 Write your ideas.

Things I wear to be warm ....

Things I wear to be cool ....

2 My new words! Draw and write.

....

3 My favorite words in this unit! Write.

....

11 Why do we travel?

1 Draw or write.

What do you know?

2 What do you learn about in this unit? Circle and write.

Who Why What travel study live

.... we ....

3 11-1 BBC What floats? Watch the video and circle.

feather Miranda paper stone

A boat floats.

A motorbike sinks.

4 What floats and sinks? Draw or write.

It floats.	It sinks.

Vocabulary 1

1 Find and circle.

boat ~~drive~~ fly helicopter motorcycle
ride sail subway train

T	D	R	I	V	E	A	D	M	W
E	F	I	H	H	E	Q	F	O	E
R	U	D	A	A	B	O	A	T	Y
B	P	E	Q	Y	T	Z	U	O	H
G	L	W	W	F	R	X	Y	R	J
A	S	U	B	W	A	Y	O	C	K
X	J	M	P	S	I	U	P	Y	C
S	A	I	L	Z	N	O	L	C	O
V	N	N	O	B	X	H	F	L	Y
H	E	L	I	C	O	P	T	E	R

2 Read and circle.

1 **ride / drive**

a bike
a motorcycle
a scooter

2 **fly / drive**

a bus
a car
a train

3 **drive / fly**

a helicopter
a plane

4 **sail / fly**

a boat

3 Listen. Then choose and write.

142

boat drive fly helicopter ~~motorcycle~~
ride sail subway train

I Sail, Ride, Drive, and Fly!

I ride my [1] motorcycle . I [2] .... my bike.
Riding is really what I like.
I [3] .... my car. I drive my [4] ....
But I go on the [5] .... in the rain.
A [6] .... ? Yes, I can fly.
And in a plane, I [7] .... high.
Then I go on the ocean. I hope I float!
As I [8] .... my [9] ....

Vocabulary challenge

4 Follow the lines and match. Then write.

Look! This .... is orange.

This .... is white and blue.

1 truck
2 taxi
3 tram
4 van

This is a white ....

This is a red ....

Story 1

1 Listen and check (✓).

143

1

2

3

4

2 Who says it? Read and match.

Oh, no, where's Patch?

This isn't a fish!

What are you doing there, Patch?

3 What toys do you travel with? Think and draw.

Grammar 1

🙂	☹️
I'm riding a bike.	I'm not playing.
She's/He's watching TV.	He/She isn't swimming.
You/We/They're having lunch.	You/We/They aren't drawing.

1 144 **Listen and number.**

a

b

c

d

e

2 **Look at Activity 1. Read and write the letters.**

1 She's sailing on a boat. *e*
2 You're floating on the water. ....
3 We're traveling on the train. ....
4 They're playing at the beach. ....
5 I'm riding my scooter. ....

3 Read and circle.

1 Patch **is** / **are** falling from the helicopter.
2 Marcia **isn't** / **aren't** sailing.
3 The children **are** / **is** riding their bikes.
4 We **aren't** / **isn't** going on a train.
5 I **'m** / **are** driving my toy car.
6 I **isn't** / **'m not** swimming.

4 Look, choose, and write.

aren't flying **driving** **flying** ~~**isn't**~~ **isn't**
riding **sailing** ~~**swimming**~~

1 She isn't sailing.
She's swimming .

2 He's .... a bike.
He .... flying.

3 We're .... in a plane.
We .... in a helicopter.

4 They aren't .... a truck.
They're .... in a boat.

Vocabulary 2

1 What's next? Write the missing numbers.

1	21	22	23	....	25
2	15	25	....	45	55
3	100	80	60	40	....
4	35	50	65	....	95

2 Make a number puzzle for your friends.

....

3 Read, choose, and write.

dangerous fast modern ~~old-fashioned~~ safe slow

1

This way to travel isn't modern. It's [1] old-fashioned . It isn't fast. It's [2] .... Is it [3] .... ? Yes, maybe it is on a windy day.

2

This way to travel is [4] .... It isn't slow. It's very [5] .... It isn't dangerous. It's [6] ....

4 Listen and draw lines.

145

5 Match the opposites.

1	safe	a	cool
2	fast	b	dangerous
3	modern	c	old-fashioned
4	big	d	slow
5	warm	e	small

Story 2

1 Read and match.

How do they get to school?

1	Lilly	a	walks to school.
2	Javier	b	takes the school bus.
3	Alex	c	goes by car.

2 Listen and circle.

146

Alex

Javier

Lilly

1 **Alex / Lilly**

2 **Javier / Lilly**

3 **Lilly / Alex**

4 **Javier / Alex**

5 **Alex / Lilly**

6 **Javier / Alex**

3 What's your favorite way to travel? Draw.

Grammar 2

We **can go to the** beach!
We **can go by** car/bike/train.
We **can go on** foot.
We **can walk**/**run**/**fly**.

1 Listen and check (✓).

147

1

3

2

4

2 Look at Activity 1. Read and circle.

1 We can go **by** / **to** the mountains.
2 We can go **on** / **by** train.
3 We can go **fly** / **walk** up the mountain.
4 We can go to the lake **by** / **on** foot.
5 We can **swim** / **run** in the lake.

3 Choose and write.

by on ~~to~~ to

1 Let's go ....to.... school.
2 We can go .... bus.
3 After school, we can go .... the park.
4 Yes, we can go .... foot.

How **can** we go to the beach?

We **can** go by bus.

We **can't** go by bike.

4 Look and complete.

1 Sara .... go to school by bike.

2 She .... go to the lake by ....

3 Marcus .... go to the store by taxi.

4 He .... go to the .... by car.

5 Write for you.

1 I can go to school ....

2 I can go to the store ....

3 I can go to my grandparents' house ....

6 Write. Then ask your friend.

How .... you go to the park?

I .... go ....

Phonics

1 Trace the letters.

qu x y

2 Listen and say. Then write *qu* or *y*.

148

1 q u een

3 __ __ iet

5 __ __ estion

2 __ ellow

4 __ ogurt

6 __ oung

3 Match and say. Write *x*.

1

2

3

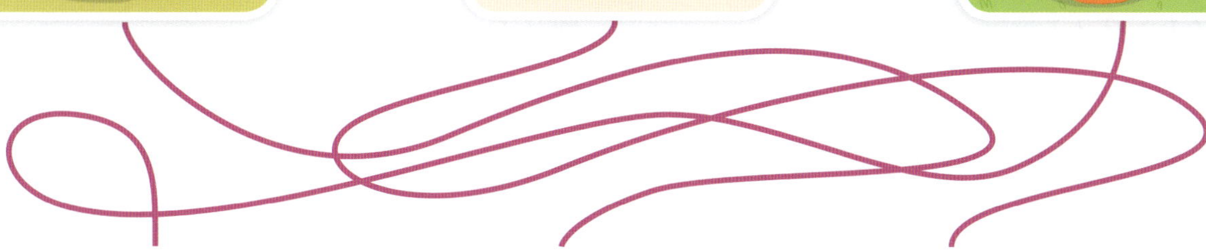

a fo __

b bo __

c si __

Now I Know

1 Find, read, and color.

Color the subway gray. Color the motorcycle red. Color the boat blue.
Color the helicopter orange. Color the train green.

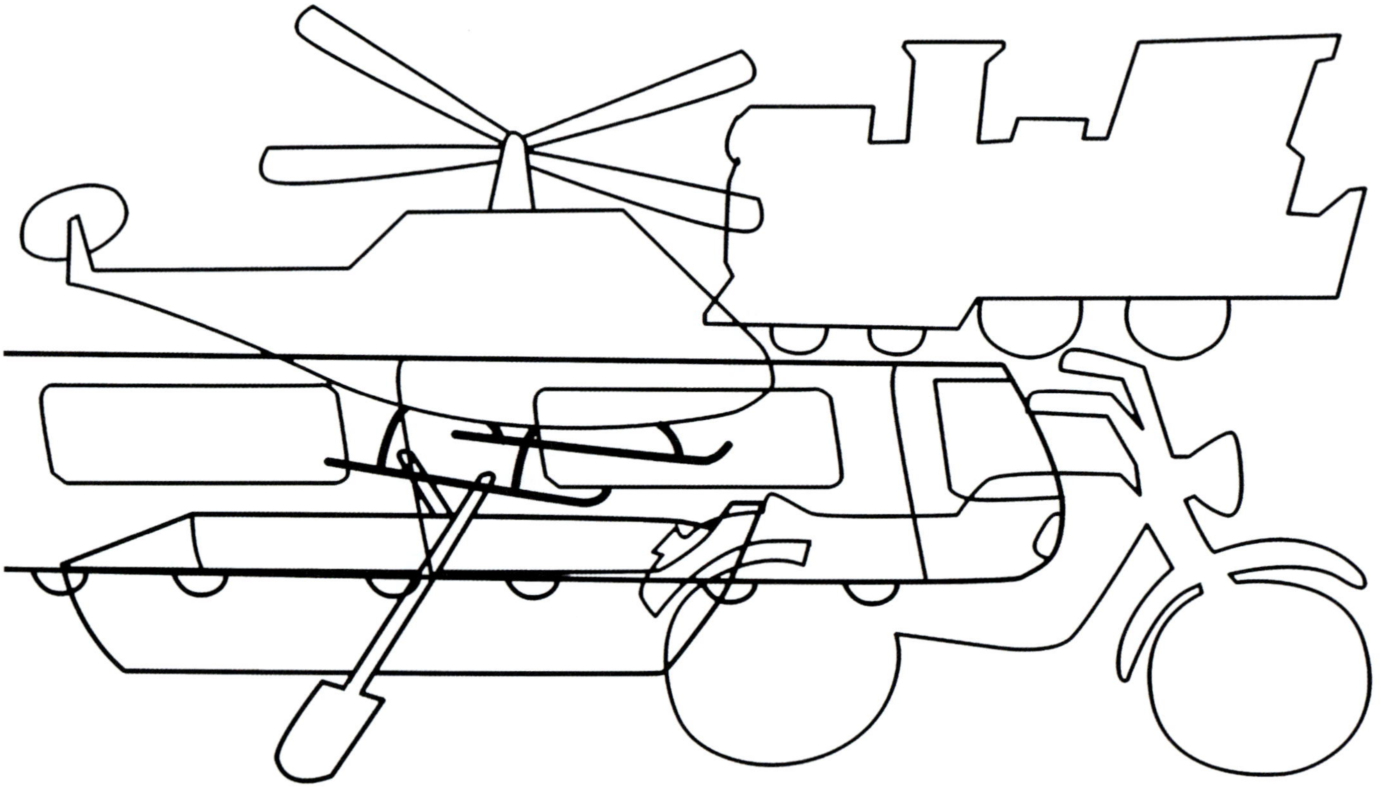

2 Write the missing letters.

1 You r __ __ e a motorcycle.
2 You d __ __ __ e a car.
3 You f __ __ a helicopter.
4 You s __ __ __ a boat.

3 Order the letters. Write the words.

1 f / a / s / e

.... → s / n / a / g / r / o / u / d / e ....

2 s / t / a / f

.... → w / o / l / s ....

3 r / e / m / o / n / d

.... → d / o / l s / h / i / n / f / o / e / d / a .... - ....

4 Look, choose, and write.

's sailing watching

can idea We

He [1] .... swimming.

He isn't [2] .... TV.

The boat is [3] ....

We [4] .... go to the park.

Great [5] .... !

[6] .... can go by bike.

Things I learn

1 Write your ideas.

Where do you travel? to school ....

How do you travel to these places? ....

2 My new words! Draw and write.

....

3 My favorite words in this unit! Write.

My three favorite words in this unit are:

....

12 Where do we live?

1 Draw or write.

What do you know?

2 What do you learn about in this unit? Circle and write.

street **home** **school** **where** **when** **how**

Our .... and .... things are.

3 ▶ 12-1 BBC What things do you hear? Watch the video and check (✓).

- shoe box ☐
- crayons ☐
- scissors ☐
- glue ☐
- string ☐

- pens ☐
- coloured paper ☐
- ruler ☐
- sticky tape ☐

4 ▶ 12-1 BBC Watch the video again. Number the sentences in order.

.... Paint the box.

.... Put the people in the room.

.... Make the furniture.

...1... Find a box.

.... Put the furniture in the room.

Vocabulary 1

1 Look and circle.

1

closet / refrigerator

3

stove / bathtub

5

couch / lamp

7

lamp / stove

2

bookcase / sink

4

couch / closet

6

sink / bathtub

8

bookcase / refrigerator

2 Read and match.

1 There's a bookcase in my
2 The bathtub is in the
3 My clothes are in my
4 The refrigerator is in the
5 I like to sit on the
6 I wash my hands in the

a couch.
b sink.
c bathroom.
d bedroom.
e kitchen.
f closet.

3 Read, choose, and write. Then listen.

149

~~bathtub~~ bookcase closet couch lamp refrigerator sink stove

In the bathroom, a [1] b athtu b and [2] s .... k.
In the bathroom, I brush my teeth.
In my bedroom, a [3] c .... t and bed.
In the bedroom, I go to sleep.
In the living room, a [4] b .... e, [5] c .... h, and [6] l .... p.
In the living room, I like to read.
In the kitchen, a [7] r .... r and [8] s .... e.
In the kitchen, I cook and eat!

Vocabulary challenge

4 Write the missing letters.

chest of drawers cushion rug vase

v __ s __

c __ s h __ __ n

c h __ s t __ f d r __ w __ __ s

r __ g

5 Look at Activity 4. Read and write.

1 We can put flowers in a ....
2 I keep my clothes in a ....
3 There's a .... on the couch.
4 There's a .... on the floor.

Story 1

1 150 **Listen and circle T (true) or F (false).**

1	T	F	4	T	F	7	T	F
2	T	F	5	T	F	8	T	F
3	T	F	6	T	F			

2 **Read and match.**

1 

2 

3 

a I live with my family in a ger.

b It's very hot in my country, so I live under the ground.

c My home is on the Amazon River.

3 151 **Listen and say.**

4 **What do you like about each house? Think and write.**

Yumi's house: You can catch fish ....

Sarnai's house: ....

Izem's house: ....

Grammar 1

Are you sleep**ing**? **Yes**, I **am**. / **No**, I**'m not**.

Is he watch**ing** TV? **Yes**, he **is**.

Is she tak**ing** a shower? **No**, she **isn't**.

Are they listen**ing** to music? **Yes**, they **are**. / **No**, they **aren't**.

1 Look at the pictures. Write the answers.

1 Maria, are you riding your bike? No, I'm not .
2 Is the girl swimming? ....
3 Is she playing with her hula-hoop? ....
4 Are the dogs playing with a ball? ....
5 Are the kittens listening to music? ....

2 Look at Activity 1. Write the correct form of *be* + verb. Say the answers.

1 Are the dogs jumping (jump)?
2 .... the girl .... (watch TV)?
3 Maria, ... you .... (have fun)?
4 .... the kittens .... (swim)?

What are you wearing?
Where do you live?
Who do you live with?
When do you go to bed?
How many brothers do you have?

3 Listen and check (✓).

152

1

2

3

4

5

4 Write. Use question words from the grammar box.

1 .... do you live?
2 .... do you wake up?
3 .... do you get to school?
4 .... do you do after school?
5 .... do you play with?

5 Think and answer.

1 What's your favorite color? ....
2 How many brothers or sisters do you have? ....
3 Who's your favorite teacher? ....

Vocabulary 2

1 Find and circle the house and home words.

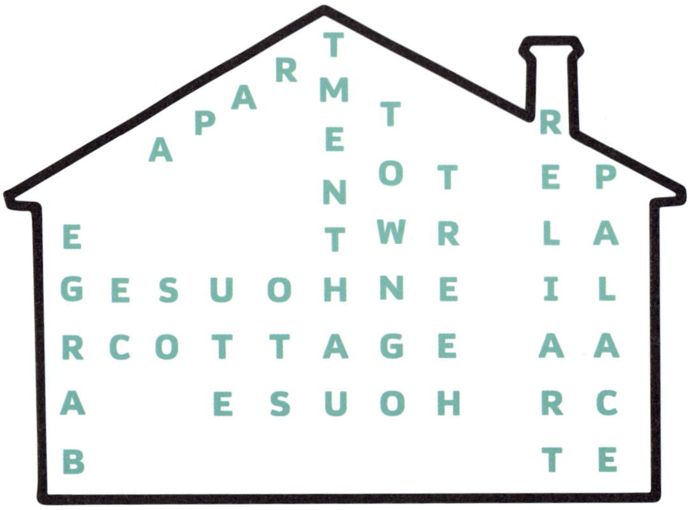

2 Look at the pictures and the letters. Write the words.

1 

____ _____

r e t e
e h u s o

2 

____

r e t
r i l a

3 

______

c a l a p e

4 

____

o t a g
e c t

3 Read, choose, and write.

apartment barge
palace trailer
tree house

What house do we live in?

1 We aren't a king and queen. We don't live in a ....
2 We don't like water. We don't live on a ....
3 We don't live in an .... in the city.
4 We don't live up a tree in a ....
5 We live in a house with wheels. We live in a ....

4 Look, read, and match.

beach house dog house greenhouse lighthouse

1

2

3

4

5 Look at Activity 4. Read and write.

1 This is a house that our dog sleeps in. ....
2 This is where we go in the summer. ....
3 This is where we grow flowers and vegetables. ....
4 This has a light to show ships where to sail. ....

Story 2

1 Read and circle.

1 Daniel lives in a **palace** / **house**.
2 His favorite place is his **trailer** / **tree house**.
3 Daniel and Maria **play** / **sleep** in the tree house.

2 Listen and number.

153

3 Where do you play? Draw and write.

4 Circle the things you like in the story.

cold beans hammock
ice cream pizza
toys tree house

Grammar 2

Where's the spider? It's **on** Tommy's head.

in **under** **next to** **in front of** **behind**

1 Read and circle the words that describe where the frog is.

Where's the frog? It's in the box. Oh, no! It's behind the box. Can you see it? Oh, but now it's in front of the box. Where's the frog now? There. It's next to the box, and now it's under the box. Can you catch it? Yes! Now the frog is in the box again.

2 Number the pictures to match the order in Activity 1.

 1

 ☐

 ☐

 ☐

 ☐

 ☐

Is it in the bathtub? **Yes**, it **is**. / **No**, it **isn't**.

3 Look, read, and circle.

1 Where's the kitten? It's **in** / **under** the bed.

2 The kitten is **in** / **on** the backpack!

3 Is the kitten next to the ball? **Yes, it is.** / **No, it isn't.**

4 Is the kitten **in front of** / **behind** the lamp? Yes, it is.

5 The kitten is **behind** / **in front of** the TV!

4 Look, choose, and write.

behind	in	in front of
it isn't	under	Where's

Alicia: [1] .... Tim?

Pablo: Tim's in his bed.

Alicia: Where's the ball?

Pablo: It's [2] .... the bed.

Alicia: Is the robot under the bed?

Pablo: No, [3] .... The robot is [4] .... the bookcase. It's [5] .... Tim's shoe!

Alicia: Oh! And the clock is [6] .... the lamp.

Phonics

1 Trace the letters.

z zz ss

2 154 Listen and say. Then write *z*, *zz*, or *ss*.

1 __ebra

3 bu__ __

5 hi__ __

2 dre__ __

4 __ero

6 fi__ __

3 Draw and say.

z	zz	ss

Now I Know

1 Read and sort.

apartment bathroom bedroom bookcase
closet house kitchen lamp townhouse

Rooms	Furniture	Where we live

2 Read and circle.

1 My teacher **are** / **is** reading in the living room.
2 You **is** / **are** watching TV in the kitchen.
3 **Is** / **Are** Sam watching TV in his bedroom?
4 I'm **eat** / **eating** breakfast in the kitchen.

3 Write the words in order to make questions.

1 in / Is / the / the / stove .... kitchen?
2 the / refrigerator / Is / in / the .... bedroom?
3 under / Is / the / lamp / the .... table?
4 the / in / Is / front / toy car / of / the .... window?

4 Look and write the answers to Activity 3.

1 Yes, ...
2 ....
3 No, ...
4 ....

5 Read and write. Ask and answer in pairs.

What When Where Who

1 .... do you go to school with?
2 .... is your favorite movie?
3 .... do you have lunch?
4 .... do you play soccer?

Who do you go to school with?

I go to school with my sister.

Things I learn

1 Write your answers.

1 What kind of house do you live in? ....
2 What's your favorite room? ....

2 My new words! Draw and write.

....

3 My favorite words in this unit! Write.

My three favorite words in this unit are:

....

Pearson Education Limited
KAO TWO
KAO Park
Hockham Way
Harlow, Essex
CM17 9SR
England
and Associated Companies throughout the world.

www.English.com

First published 2019

ISBN: 978-1-292-21931-8

Set in Daytona Pro Semibold 12pt over 17pt

Printed and bound by L.E.G.O. S.p.A. Italy

Image Credit(s):
123RF.com: 86, 100, 105, 105, 122, 136, Acceptphoto 55, Aleksey Boldin 7, 19, Alexander Makarov 132, Alinute 120, Andersonrise 75, 75, 87, Andrey Kiselev 75, 87, Andrii Klemenchenko 136, Andriy Popov 94, Antonfoltin 35, Arina Zaiachin 38, Belchonock 55, 55, Blueperfume 75, Brainsil 86, Coprid 108, Darios 59, Dmitry Rukhlenko 154, Donka Zheleva 131, Doomu 8, Dulcenombre Maria Rubia Ramirez 133, Efired 59, Eriklam 48, familylifestyle 131, 132, 143, Filipe Frazao 161, Frantysek 106, Gennadiy Shelest 154, Golubsergei 111, Inga Nielsen 112, Iriana88w 170, Irina Schmidt 126, Irina Ukrainets 82, Irochka 7, Jacek Chabraszewski 10, 106, Jaroonrat Vitoosuwan 159, Jenifoto 33, Jose Manuel Gelpi Diaz 75, 87, Jovannig 76, Jules_Kitano 117, Kai Chiang 66, kamolrat 133, Lammeyer 165, Laures 82, Leung Cho Pan 75, 87, lightmoon 133, Llia Starikov 136, Lopolo 92, Loraliu 49, 58, Magone 37, Magraphics 159, Maksym Narodenko 103, Maksym Yemelyanov 159, Margie Hurwich 64, Martin Damen 103, 106, Mch67 56, Mezzotint123rf 95, Michael Simons 66, Mohammed Anwarul Kabir Choudhury 137, Nalinratana Phiyanalinmat 132, Nanisimova 142, Nataliia Prokofyeva 74, Natika 103, 103, 104, 108, Nerthuz 82, Nito500 8, Nitr 47, Olechowski 146, Olegdudko 7, Olga Kriger 94, Peterm 94, Popovaphoto 142, Rafael Ben-Ari 52, 58, Randy Harris 47, 58, Rawpixel 154, 154, Rido 64, Robertsre 108, Roblan 30, Roman Fernati 108, Ruslan Kudrin 140, Sam74100 90, Samuel Micut 93, 100, Scanrail 154, Sergey Jarochkin 7, Sergey Kolesnikov 107, Sergii Kateryniuk 51, Sergii Telesh 107, Sergiy Kuzmin 117, Sharlotta Ulrikh 70, Siraphol 8, 131, Sirichai Asawalapsakul 107, Steven Heap 52, 58, 58, Stieberszabolcs 47, 49, 59, Sval 48, Svetlana Voronina 132, Thampapon Otavorn 150, Tsekhmister 52, Utima 107, Vadim Yerofeyev 30, Vereshchagin Dmitry 82, Vitalii Tiahunov 117, 128, Vitalina Rybakova 19, Vladimir Nenov 128, Volodymyr Goinyk 52, 58, Warongdech Thaiwatcharamas 107, Warrengoldswain 75, Wavebreak Media Ltd 37, 38, 100, Wavebreakmediamicro 42, Wilawan Khasawong 120, Wong Yu Liang 22, Yiorgosgr 74, Ysign 47, 58, 59, Yurakp 103, Yuriy Shevtsov 75, Вадим Захарищев 140; **Alamy Stock Photo:** AKP Photos 10, Alexander Mychko 112, Ammentorp Photography 95, Andy Dean Photography 69, Anna Kucherova 103, Arcaid Images 170, Arco Images GmbH 84, Aurora Photos 21, Birgit Reitz-Hofmann 7, 10, 36, Blickwinkel 56, 97, Brian_Kinney 104, Canva Pty Ltd 120, Cultura Creative (RF) 37, Daisy-Daisy 89, David L.Moore 154, David Lee 36, 106, 111, Denis Crawford 133, Dimitar Todorov 92, Dmitriy Shironosov 70, Dorling Kindersley Ltd 133, enache sebastian 133, Evan Sklar 76, Eyesite 46, Franzfoto.com 35, FS-Stock 101, Helen Sessions 120, Hero Images Inc. 70, 79, 139, ImageBROKER 76, ImageDB 7, Images By Kenny 86, Indiapicture 12, Jacek Kadaj 160, Joe Fairs 22, Juice Images 126, 136, Juniors Bildarchiv GmbH 49, Kitch Bain 8, Krzysztof Serafiński 52, 58, Kuttig - People 100, Luis Torres 9, Lumi Images 120, Markus Mainka 114, Martin Lee 103, MBI 86, 93, Michael Diggin 82, Murray Hayward 101, Nick Moore 120, Novarc Images 64, 73, 73, OJO Images Ltd 95, 101, Owen Derrick 35, Patchanu Noree 36, PhotoAlto 139, PhotosIndia.com LLC 143, Radius Images 153, Rawpixel Ltd 126, Rick & Nora Bowers 35, Robert de Jong 52, 58, Robertharding 161, ScotStock 114, Sergey Karpov 148, Sergey Novikov 97, Sergii Kateryniuk 102, Shotshop GmbH 86, Sport In Pictures 96, StellaPhotography 30, Stephen Flint 13, Sunshine 100, Sylvie Bouchard 86, Tetra Images 12, Tetra Images, LLC 122, Tim Hill 112, Valentyn Volkov 103, Veeravong Komalamena 104, Vincent O'Byrne 39, Visuals Stock 124, Wavebreak Media ltd 46, 83, Westend61 GmbH 100, 136, Zahra Harira 114, Zero Creatives 49, Zoonar GmbH 22, 152; **BBC Worldwide Learning:** BBC - Co-Branded Products 4, 18, 32, 46, 60, 74, 88, 102, 116, 130, 144, 158; **Getty Images:** Ariel Skelley 64, BananaStock 33, Bartosz Hadyniak 7, Bellurget Jean Louis 124, By Mira 93, Cargo 63, Comstock 120, Daniela Duncan 90, Dave King 105, David Sacks 133, Davidf 64, Dev Carr 89, Dianne Avery Photography 79, 79, Dorioconnell 49, Duncan1890 63, Energyy 61, FatCamera 100, Gldburger 105, Grafissimo 152, Hill Street Studios 95, Hugh Sitton 7, Imazins/Plan Shoot 100, Imgorthand 139, James Osmond 148, Jasmin Merdan 64, JazzIRT 159, Joseph Sohm-Visions of America 55, 55, Juanmonino 120, Jupiterimages 33, Kgfoto 49, Kirin_photo 84, Krimzoya 63, Lillian Suwanrumpha 96, Loonger 161, Oleksandr Hrytsiv 122, Peter Cade 37, Randy Faris 7, Rick Gomez 82, romrodinka 126, Ryan McVay 124, Savoilic 22, Stills 37, SusanadelCampoPhoto 152, SVGiles 76, Teresa Short 21, Tim Dolan Photography 152, Vgajic 100, Voren1 55, Wavebreakmedia 83, Westend61 97, 122, Xavier ROSSI 133, Zero Creatives 84, 93; **Imagestate:** Phovoir 10; **Pearson Education Ltd:** Alice McBroom 12, Cheuk-king Lo 86, Coleman Yuen 146, Lord and Leverett 66, Studio 8 19, 79, 120, Trevor Clifford 92, 92, 114, Tudor Photography 56; **Shutterstock.com:** 78, 1595666 76, 1701346 103, A40757 165, Adisa 114, Africa Studio 17, 33, 42, 55, 75, 82, 103, 104, 112, 114, Akepong Srichaichana 114, Alena Ozerova 139, Alex Poison 164, Alex Staroseltsev 114, All About Space 159, Alla Shcherbak 61, Amble Design 89, Amy Myers 86, Ana Blazic Pavlovic 76, Anastasiia Skorobogatova 114, Andresr 66, Andrey Arkusha 123, Andrey Burstein 123, Andrey_Popov 102, Andrienko Anastasiya 142, Anna Golant 133, Anna Sedneva 108, Ant Cooper 46, 48, Anton Boldak 161, Artsandra 63, Atlaspix 164, Auremar 94, Balenopix 86, BasPhoto 133, Batmanv 13, Benjamas11 47, Blend Images 33, 42, BlueOrange Studio 89, Bombaert Patrick 82, Brandy Wright 75, 87, Brian A Jackson 89, BrunoWeltmann 38, Brykaylo Yuriy 154, Byjeng 159, Carballo 12, Catalin Petolea 56, 61, 103, Chainarong Suriya 47, 58, Chamille White 112, Christopher Meder 36, chuyuss 131, Clarst5 48, Cloki 103, 112, Dado Photos 105, Darren Hubley 94, Decha Laoharuengrongkun 148, Denis Dryashkin 107, Denis Kuvaev 96, Denis Rozhnovsky 10, DGLimages 79, Didesign021 42, Diego Cervo 70, Digital Media Pro 42, Dimedrol68 75, Dina Uretski 100, Dionisvera 106, Diyana Dimitrova 133, Doglikehorse 70, Dreamer Company 82, Dudarev Mikhail 92, Dusit Paichalerm 137, Edhar 94, Edward Lara 79, Elena Elisseeva 102, Emin Ozkan 102, Epiximages 79, Eric Isselee 48, 48, 48, 52, 55, 58, 133, ErickN 22, Ericsmandes 96, ESB Professional 82, 122, Esin Deniz 55, EtiAmmos 105, Evannovostro 30, Evgeniia Trushkova 13, EvgeniiAnd 66, Evgeny Karandaev 102, Fh Photo 84, Flashon Studio 38, FloridaStock 165, foodonwhite 114, Fotokostic 94, Fotosv 142, Four Oaks 52, 58, Freer 114, Frolphy 94, 100, Gajus 132, Gaschwald 35, 35, Gelpi JM 38, 39, Gencho Petkov 102, Gigio Bertachi 58, Gines Romero 100, Gladskikh Tatiana 10, Goodluz 61, 148, 152, Gopfaster 137, 140, Gpointstudio 123, Graja 133, Greenland 100, Gregory Gerber 47, Guentermanaus 161, Guitar photographer 51, Henry Steven 136, Hong Vo 114, Horsemen 58, Hurst Photo 114, Iakov Filimonov 69, 72, 97, IamDOT 106, IB Photography 17, Inc 100, Inna Zueva Nikolaevna 66, Isarescheewin 161, Iuliia Tarabanova 13, Ivan Marjanovic 51, Jack Frog 64, Jack Shiffer 21, Jacob Lund 111, Jag_cz 58, 59, JaysonPhotography 49, Jeff Gynane 164, Jerry Horbert 133, Jiri Hera 36, Joat 19, Joe Ravi 22, Jon Manjeot 35, 37, Just dance 122, Juthamat98 117, 128, Kaband 150, Karina Bakalyan 133, Karkas 131, 133, 137, Karlowac 159, Karnizz 146, Kenishirotie 38, Khram 51, Kichigin 165, Kitch Bain 17, KK Art and Photography 39, Kletr 17, 19, Kobby Dagan 82, Koldunov 61, Konstantin Gushcha 114, Kurhan 38, Larich 22, Lenasirena 19, Lepas 103, Lipatova Maryna 76, Lisa F. Young 106, Littlekidmoment 64, Lopolo 69, 154, Madlen 19, Maggy Meyer 36, Maks Narodenko 102, Mali lucky 106, Mangojuicy 10, 123, Margo Harrison 7, Markus Mainka 108, Mario7 106, Maryna Kulchytska 142, Mathom 10, Matthias Pahl 30, Mauro Rodrigues 120, Max Blender 3D 159, Max Lashcheuski 19, Max Topchii 82, Maya Kruchankova 101, Mcimage 33, Mega Pixel 8, Mezzotint 96, Michael Dechev 131, 143, Mihai Blanaru 86, Mike Flippo 102, Milart 108, 111, MilsiArt 52, Miroshnichenko Tetiana 8, Mo Wu 56, MoinMoin 102, MBI 33, 61, 64, 66, 66, 66, 70, 79, 94, 112, Monsterstock 112, monticello 114, Morgenstjerne 106, Moving Moment 114, mTaira 94, NadyaEugene 89, Naluwan 12, Nattesha 52, Nattika 106, Niceregionpics 8, Nico Traut 165, Nikifor Todorov 58, Nikkytok 38, Nikshor 7, Nipaporn Panyacharoen 106, Nomad_Soul 137, Oleg suhenco 10, Oleksiy Mark 94, Olga Nayashkova 19, Olga Popova 131, 140, 143, Olga_i 36, Ozgur Coskun 83, Panbazil 48, Pao Laroid 9, Perla Berant Wilder 22, Petr Malyshev 106, Phloen 49, 49, Photo Melon 22, Photocrea 107, Photomaster 55, 55, Picturepartners 61, 61, Pressmaster 83, 84, Pumidol 19, Pyzata 154, Raisa Kanareva 75, Reinhold Leitner 47, 58, Rob Marmion 100, Robert Pernell 146, Rodolfo Arpia 12, Romakoma 21, 21, Ron Zmiri 164, Ruslan Kudrin 131, Saaras 39, Samokhin 106, Sand Storm Studio 117, Sarahbean 42, Schubbel 52, 58, Selma ARSLAN 120, Seregam 10, Serg78 105, Sergio33 19, 108, Sergiy Kuzmin 117, Shawn Hempel 103, shiva3d 120, Shutterstudio 84, Shyamalamuralinath 8, Skyfish 52, SMAK_Photo 117, Smalldaruma 136, Smereka 46, 49, SnowWhiteimages 78, Somen 142, Spaxiax 103, SpeedKingz 69, StanislauV 128, StevenRussellSmithPhotos 133, Studio KIWI 140, SuzanaT 105, Svetislav1944 9, Syda Productions 13, Sylv1rob1 61, Taiftin 140, Taste it 58, Tetyana Kaganska 111, Thechatat 92, Thorsten Rust 152, Tim UR 103, TinnaPong 36, Tischenko Irina 105, Tompet 48, Tono Balaguer 46, 93, Topseller 105, Tpfeller 117, Travnikiov Studio 148, Trevor Clifford 102, Vadarshop 30, Valentina Razumova 90, Valentyn Volkov 46, 107, Valua Vitaly 154, Veronica Louro 13, Viktar Malyshchyts 102, Vovan 142, Warren Metcalf 35, Wavebreakmedia 23, 33, 66, WithGod 56, XiXinXing 136, Yellow Cat 9, YK 19, 22, 30, Yuliya Yesina 38, Zeljko Radojko 49, Zurijeta 61, 64, 64, 79.

Cover Images: *Front:* **Getty Images:** Loop Images/Leila Balin

Illustrated by Alternative View Studios Ltd p.4, 17; Charlie Alder (Bright Group) p.119; Nila Aye (Meilkjohn) p.8, 9, 17, 19, 27, 31, 33, 35, 39(schoolgirl), 40(Ex.2), 41, 42, 44, 45(Ex. 1), 51(Ex. 4), 67(main scene), 69(frame 1), 73(Ex.2), 78(Ex. 1), 84(Ex. 5), 85(Ex. 2), 95, 112, 118, 122, 125, 146, 162, 167(grammar box), 168(Ex. 3); Martyn Cain (Beehive Illustration) p.5(Ex. 2), 19(Ex. 3), 23(Ex. 4), 24, 49, 51(Ex. 5), 53(Ex. 4), 80(Ex. 1), 81(Ex. 4), 84(Ex. 6), 85(Ex. 2), 105, 111, 113(Ex. 3), 130, 141(Ex. 2), 163, 169; Mattia Cerato (Mbartists) p.40(Ex.1); Livia Coloji (The Organisation) p.91(Ex. 1); Gareth Conway (The Bright Agency) p.138; Sara Lyn Cramb (Astound) p50(Ex.2), 55(Ex. 2b); Camilla Galindo (Beehive Illustration) in various styles p.11, 15, 26(Ex. 2 speech bubble artwork), 29, 34(Ex. 3), 41(Ex. 1), 43(Ex. 3), 44, 57, 65(Ex. 4), 67(1–6), 69(frame 2–4), 71, 72, 78(Ex. 2), 80(Ex. 2), 85(Ex. 3), 90(Ex. 3), 91(Ex. 2), 94, 97, 99(Ex. 3), 101(Ex. 2), 108(Ex. 1), 113(Ex. 2), 141(Ex. 3); Francesca Gambatesa (MMB Creative) p.5, 10, 23, 30, 45(Ex. 2&4), 50(Ex.1), 62, 81(Ex. 3), 87(Ex. 2), 90(Ex. 4), 99(Ex. 3), 104, 109 (Ex. 5), 115, 121, 134, 135, 142, 156, 167(Ex. 2); Keri Green (Beehive Illustration) p.4(Ex. 2 objects), 16, 44(Ex. 1), 58, 73(Ex. 4); James Loram (Lemonade Illustration) 77; Hannah Marks (Astound) p.110(Ex. 1); Kasia Nowowiejska (Good Illustration) p.12; Emma Nyari (Beehive Illustration) p.6, 13, 32, 34(Ex. 5), 36, 37, 39(Ex. 3 table), 41(Ex. 2), 43(Ex. 2), 66, 70, 88, 99(Ex. 2), 127, 153, 155; Caroline Romanet (Advocate) p.54; Sussana Rumiz (Lemonade Illustration) p.6, 14, 20, 25, 28, 38, 39(cat), 44(Ex.2), 48, 53(Ex. 2), 59, 61, 65(Ex.3), 72, 83, 87(Ex. 3), 93, 98, 101(Ex. 2), 108(Ex. 3), 109(Ex. 4), 126, 129, 137, 149(Ex. 4), 151, 157, 168(Ex. 4), 171; Glen Thomas (Bright Group) p.147, 149(Ex. 3); Emma Trihart (Bright Group) p.166; Ghyslaine Vaysset (Astound) p.26; Richard Watson (Bright Group) p.16, 55(Ex. 2a), 167(Ex. 1); Annie Wilkinson (Advocate Art) p.68.

FSC
www.fsc.org
MIX
Paper from responsible sources
FSC™ C128612